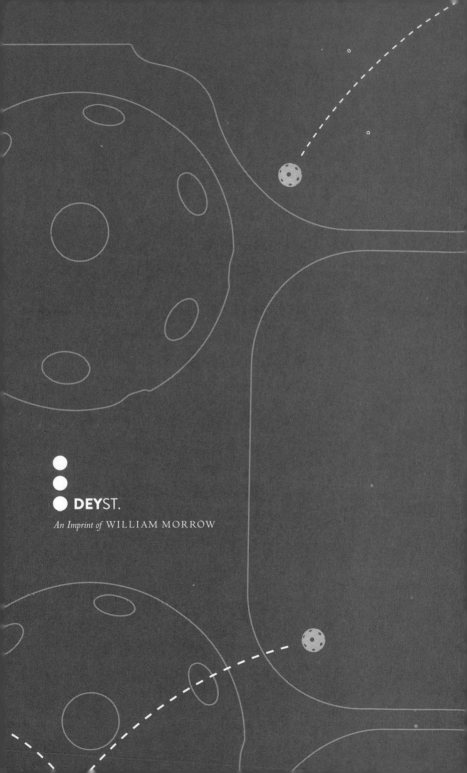

DEYST.

An Imprint of WILLIAM MORROW

PICKLEBALL
for ALL

EVERYTHING BUT
THE "KITCHEN" SINK

RACHEL SIMON

HarperCollins books may be purchased for educational, business, or sales promotional
use. For information, please e-mail the Special Markets Department at SPsales
@harpercollins.com.

FIRST EDITION

Designed by Angela Boutin

Library of Congress Cataloging-in-Publication Data has been applied for.

ISBN 978-0-06-327304-7

22 23 24 25 26   LSC   10 9 8 7 6 5 4 3 2 1

For Kurt, my partner in pickleball and life.

CONT

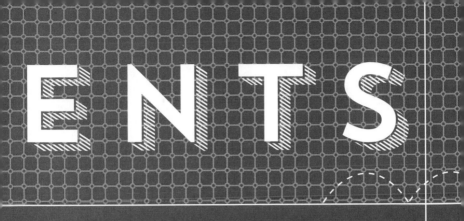

ENTS

There are countless people I've met and memories I've made—and will continue to make—thanks to pickleball. You can bet anywhere I travel, I have a paddle on hand in case I find a group looking for an extra player.

—Dave Gould, 4.0-level pickleball player

INTRODUCTION

n March 2020, Kurt (my then boyfriend and now husband) and I were spending the early days of the pandemic in the same boat as millions of other people: quarantining with our family in the North Carolina suburbs, adjusting to Zoom meetings and work-from-home life, and entertaining ourselves with marathons of *Tiger King*. We were craving new ways to pass the time and keep ourselves distracted from the increasingly frightening news, but our options were limited. Walks? Too repetitive. Board games? Too tedious. Group hangouts? Too unsafe. In other words: we were really, really, bored.

And then, at the beginning of April, Kurt's parents gifted him a set of pickleball paddles and balls for his birthday. Neither of them had any experience with the sport, but they'd heard from friends it was fun, easy to learn, and simple to set up. Besides, they reasoned, if we didn't like it, the equipment was relatively cheap— even if we only played a few rounds before tossing the paddles in the back of a closet, they'd have been worth the buy.

Kurt and I were intrigued, if skeptical. Neither of us was an athlete by any measure, and our own limited history with pickleball was relegated to middle school gym classes. Still, it *did* seem entertaining, and with our Netflix queue dwindling alarmingly fast, we knew we could benefit from a new activity. So, after work the next day, we marched out to the driveway, set up a makeshift court with chalk and tape, and googled "how to play pickleball." A few quick tutorials later, we had a vague sense of the game, a new definition of the word *kitchen*, and a desire to just get out there and try things out for ourselves.

Were we any good that first time? Absolutely not. Between my badly aimed serves and Kurt's too-fast returns, the two of us spent the greater portion of that inaugural pickleball game in a perpetual sprint around the court, more focused on gathering far-flung balls than actually scoring points. Even our poor car, parked over to the side, suffered a beating during the game thanks to our wayward hits.

But man, did we have a blast. Despite our inexperience and lack of athletic ability, we found ourselves loving every aspect of the sport, from readying our serves to judging each shot's merit to eking out the occasional long-lasting volley. The small size of the court made things simple to navigate, while the flatness of the paddles gave our swings a wonderfully lightweight, airy feel. There was no drag like in tennis, echo like in racquetball, or easy misses like in Ping-Pong. Pickleball, it seemed, was the best of all worlds—and with so few supplies needed, we could play it wherever we wanted, whenever we wanted.

Which, naturally, we did. Over the next several weeks, Kurt and I became pickleball enthusiasts, playing near-daily games after work together, often with his parents joining us for doubles. Off Amazon, we ordered a net and some extra paddles; from YouTube, we learned a few more rules and strategies, some of which we actually managed to put to use. By the end of the month, the four of us were so into the game that we even set up our own mini pickleball tournament, complete with team "uniforms" (that is, matching shorts and tees) and celebratory Pimm's Cup drinks. (Kurt and I won, but his parents put up a fierce competition.)

It was a great way to spend our days, but outside the bubble of our home, the situation was continuing to worsen. Across the world, the number of positive COVID-19 cases had begun to skyrocket, and hospitals were filling up distressingly fast. Masks were bought, then worn to the grocery store; groceries were bought, then washed over and over. Back in March, when Kurt and I had originally left our apartment in Brooklyn to head down to Asheville, we'd figured we'd be there for one, two weeks at most, waiting out the worst of things and heading back once the crisis had eased. Yet a month into our stay, the pandemic was raging on stronger than ever, and our optimism had started to fade into despair. With so many unknowns and new fears taking hold, all the things that had once captured our interest—TV, music, movies, games— began to feel silly and stale. Everything, that is, except pickleball.

To our surprise, pickleball offered what none of those other pastimes could: a safe, accessible, and endlessly enjoyable way for people of all different ages, body types, and fitness levels to come together. With only one or two players on each side of the court and no touching required, the game was practically tailor-made for social distancing, and since there was no formal training needed to learn the basics, anyone could participate and pick up the rules fairly quickly. Compared to other similar sports and activities, pickleball provided something fresh and inclusive, and the heightened action of each match made it far more interesting than another walk around the neighborhood or overcomplicated card game.

The more we played, the more I wondered why everyone else wasn't doing the same thing. Pickleball, it seemed to me, was the ideal sport for the unusual circumstances we were in that spring—surely, our family wasn't the only one who'd realized this, right? Turns out, we certainly were not. One Twitter search for "pickleball" later and it became clear that many other people throughout the country had also taken up the game while in quarantine, creating their own setups on driveways or tennis courts and buying equipment online. Some, I learned, had even formed casual leagues with others in their COVID bubbles, wearing gloves while competing to minimize the spreading of germs. There were parents playing with kids, teens playing with millennials, seniors playing with neighbors and friends. Everywhere I looked, pickleball was taking over, one homemade court at a time.

As a writer, I knew that I needed to share what I was seeing with more people. So, I pitched a story to the *New York Times* about pickleball's seemingly sudden rise in popularity, and how well it fit the current times. A few weeks and plenty of research later, it was in print for all to see: *Is Pickleball the Perfect Pandemic Pastime?* The answer, countless others and I knew, was yes.

In the more than two years since that article was published, I've heard from hundreds of people about their own pickleball love stories—how they started playing, what got them hooked, and all the different ways the game helped them deal with the isolation and frustrations of the pandemic. I've talked to parents who credit pickleball for getting their kids out of the house and away from screens, and eighty-year-olds who happily base their whole schedules around daily neighborhood games. I've heard from nonathletes like myself who've gotten in great shape thanks to the sport, and serious players who've started coaching others in addition to honing their own skills. I've spoken with a small-town mayor who gets to know his constituents through bouts on the court, and a man who came out of retirement to teach pickleball in prisons and jails across the country, so sure that the game would aid the inmates' physical and mental well-being. Speaking of which—when I told my therapist that I was writing this book, she revealed that she was a passionate player herself who spent her weekends playing games with friends and taking lessons offered through her town swim club. Learning that, I knew I wanted to chat with her further about the game and its benefits to players' mental health, in particular, so I set up a separate phone call with her following our appointment. On the call, Patricia—after amusingly commenting on how odd it felt to not be talking about my problems for once—told me how helpful she believes pickleball has been for players during the last few years.

"With the pandemic, we've all been so isolated, and people are looking for a sense of community," she explained. "And pickleball is perfect for that."

Additionally, she said, the game having such a low barrier to entry means that players can "feel successful at the very start," a rare and valuable thing in a world filled with challenges. (Also, she added, pickleball gets players out the house and active. "We're not sitting around drinking wine—well, later we are," she noted.)

Whether it's a therapist spending her Saturday mornings at the courts, a dad practicing drills with his daughter in the backyard, or a pro athlete traveling the country to compete in tournaments, it's undeniable how popular pickleball has become. From 2020 to 2022, the number of players in the United States grew 39.3 percent, to a total of 4.8 million people, per the Sports & Fitness Industry Association's (SFIA) 2022 Topline Participation Report.[1] There are now hundreds more courts around the country than there were just a few short years ago, including in school gyms, retirement communities, and country clubs; in some neighborhoods, new apartment complexes are being built with pickleball, not tennis, as the main outdoor court activity. Pickleball tournaments are also becoming increasingly popular, with major competitions like the U.S. Open and National Championships drawing thousands of players and fans, many of whom plan their yearly travel schedules around the often party-like events. In Atlantic City, New Jersey, a tournament set for September 2022 is expected to be the world's largest indoor competition ever, with seven thousand players predicted to attend from all over the world.[2]

Worldwide, the game is also growing at a quick pace. The International Federation of Pickleball (IFP) has seen a 360 percent increase in member countries just since 2019,[3] and players everywhere participate in overseas tournaments and clinics. In countries like Mexico and Thailand, pickleball-centric travel companies offer vacation packages where tourists can split their time between sightseeing and playing. Currently, some of the sport's top advocates are even working hard to get pickleball qualified for the 2028 Olympic Games in Los Angeles, an ambition that not long ago would have seemed far-fetched, but now is looking more and more likely to come true by the day.

And with celebrities from Kim Kardashian to Bill Gates helping the surge by sharing their love of the game on social media, it's no wonder that pickleball has been labeled the fastest-growing sport in America. Everyone wants to play—and with the game's unparalleled accessibility and ease, everyone *can*.

Unlike many other sports where factors like age, gender, or ability often act as limitations to entry, pickleball provides a refreshingly equal playing field, with opportunities for fans of all types to get involved. Any person looking to join a game can simply walk onto an open-play court at their local park or gym, without prior notice, and rotate into a match. Even total beginners are given the chance to participate, with more experienced players often voluntarily taking them under their wing to show them the ropes.

And the more players get to know each other, the more opportunities there are for friendships to develop. Tracie Holmes, a player, ambassador, and coach from Avalon, New Jersey, with whom I connected through USA Pickleball, told me that when she first moved to her neighborhood several years ago, she knew no one and struggled with the loneliness. "I moved to a new area as an older adult, and had to really start over," she explained. But once she made a local friend who happened to play pickleball, she took up the sport herself, and saw her social circle instantly widen as a result. Now she's a passionate player with multiple close friendships, all thanks to pickleball.

"There are women and men I talk to on a daily basis that I didn't know five years ago before I started playing," Holmes said, adding, "I'm a sixty-year-old woman. Who meets new friends at sixty? But pickleball has enabled that."

Gender norms, too, don't hamper pickleball's inclusive spirit, and neither does ability. Joe Sullivan, a paraplegic player and coach from Naples, Florida, said that in his experience, being in a wheelchair hasn't limited his chances to play alongside others and make new friends. "It's a very welcoming community in terms of [able-bodied] people playing with wheelchair players," he told me over the phone. "Everybody is like, 'I'll play with you, let's play!'"

"To me," he continued, "that's the magic of pickleball. And it's the same for a wheelchair player or any player."

On the competition side of the game, things are just as inclusive. At an average tournament, wheelchair players like Sullivan compete alongside able-bodied persons, ten-year-olds face off against adults, and mixed doubles matches (a.k.a. those featuring both men and women) are as widely watched as any others. It's not just professional athletes, either; the vast majority of tournament participants are casual players looking to get in some friendly competition while enjoying the significant social and entertainment benefits the days-long events have to offer.

With so much to love about the sport, it's no surprise that businesses have begun to take note. Dozens of athletic and apparel companies now produce pickleball-themed clothing and accessories, in addition to coffee mugs, throw pillows, and pretty much any other products you can think of. Brands ranging from Skechers to Volvo frequently sponsor tournaments, and the game's most well-known players have sponsorships—and big followings—of their own. TV channels, too, have hopped on the pickleball train, with networks like ESPN and the Tennis Channel now featuring coverage of the game to keep up with viewer demand.

So what's next? There's no way to know for sure, of course, but at the rate things are going, the future of pickleball certainly looks bright—even as the world's situation remains unclear. In the time since I first picked up that paddle, the pandemic hasn't ceased, and while new information and vaccines have eased many of our original fears, going back to "normal" is no longer a possibility for me, or any of us.

Although I may not have a clue what lies ahead, I *do* know that pickleball will be a big part of it. Sure, there are far more options now to entertain myself safely and connect with others than there were back in the spring of 2020. But few of them are as reliably fun, inclusive, and simple as grabbing a paddle and gearing up for a serve. I may not be a professional (or, let's be honest, anything near one), but the feeling of diving low to return a drive, or using a perfect backspin to send the ball into flight, still brings me the biggest sense of satisfaction. Pickleball is a sport that's impossible not to love, and I'm so grateful that I got over my initial skepticism all those months ago to give it the chance it deserved.

What makes it all even more enjoyable is knowing that I'm far from the only one who feels that way. When Laura Gainor, a marketing consultant to USA Pickleball (the sport's American governing body), first started getting heavily involved in the game in 2019, more than a few friends shared their doubts that the sport with the funny name would amount to anything—and that anyone under the age of sixty would want to play.

"People joked about it," Gainor recalled when we spoke. "They thought I was starting something that wasn't really gonna take off."

Three years and a few million more pickleball fans later, those friends are singing a very different tune. Now Gainor—who even moved her family from Chicago to Florida in 2021 largely because of her new community's abundance of courts and proximity to pickleball meccas like Naples and Daytona—has an inbox constantly full of requests from potential players wanting information on the game. "They're now like, 'I want to get in! I want to play!'" she said.

Part of this enthusiasm is no doubt due to the changing reputation of pickleball, from a sport many (like Gainor's friends) assumed to be solely enjoyed by senior citizens to one now played with vigor by people of every age, including kids and teens. Truly, pickleball is for all—no matter your age, gender, skill level, or anything else.

But whether you're a total newcomer or a seasoned pro, there's a lot you probably don't know about the sport, from its humble origins on an island in Washington State, to the strategies top players use to up their skills, to the impassioned efforts some fans are making to get pickleball the recognition it deserves. Because as every player knows, the world is a whole lot better when you've got a paddle, a court, and a community full of people bonded together by their love of a game.

TIMELINE

1965

PICKLEBALL IS CREATED.

Barney McCallum, Joel Pritchard, and Bill Bell invent the game on Bainbridge Island, Washington.

1972

PICKLE-BALL INC. FORMS.

The first pickleball corporation comes into existence.

1976

THE FIRST PICKLEBALL TOURNAMENT IS HELD.

More than sixty players compete in Tukwila, Washington.

1984

THE USAPA FORMS.

President and executive director Sid Williams leads the development of a rule book, ranking system, and more.

1984

THE FIRST COMPOSITE PADDLE IS CREATED.

Industrial engineer Arlen Paranto's popular prototype inspires dozens of other manufacturers worldwide.

1990

PICKLEBALL IS PLAYED IN ALL FIFTY STATES.

Tournaments begin gaining popularity across America.

1999

PICKLEBALLSTUFF.COM LAUNCHES.

The first pickleball website debuts on the Internet.

2001

PICKLEBALL JOINS THE ARIZONA SENIOR OLYMPICS.

The one-hundred-player tournament is the largest pickleball event yet, held in Surprise, Arizona.

2005

THE USAPA REBRANDS.

The new organization creates a single database of places to play pickleball nationwide.

2008

ABC'S *GOOD MORNING AMERICA* HIGHLIGHTS PICKLEBALL.

The TV segment marks the game's first mass-media exposure.

2022

PICKLEBALL IS PLAYED BY 4.8 MILLION PEOPLE.
The SFIA's annual report notes a 39.3 percent increase in players since 2020.

2021

PICKLEBALL TAKES OVER THE MEDIA.
Articles in the *New York Times*, *Vanity Fair*, the *Boston Globe*, and many other outlets aid the sport's continued growth.

2020

THE USAPA REBRANDS AGAIN.
It's now known as USA Pickleball.

2019

THE PROFESSIONAL PICKLEBALL ASSOCIATION (PPA) AND ASSOCIATION OF PICKLEBALL PROFESSIONALS (APP) FORM.
The organizations create two major tours with dozens of tournaments.

2018

THE USA PICKLEBALL NATIONAL CHAMPIONSHIPS MOVES FROM ARIZONA TO CALIFORNIA'S INDIAN WELLS TENNIS GARDEN.
It provides the biggest cash purse, $75,000, in the sport's history.

2017

THE PICKLEBALL HALL OF FAME LAUNCHES.
Inaugural inductees include the sport's three founders, with their photos displayed in Kent, Washington.

2016

THE FIRST U.S. OPEN PICKLEBALL CHAMPIONSHIPS IS HELD.
Thousands of players and fans attend the competition in Naples, Florida.

2015

PICKLEBALL HITS MORE THAN 2 MILLION PLAYERS WORLDWIDE.
Numbers of courts and tournaments continue to multiply.

2010

THE INTERNATIONAL FEDERATION OF PICKLEBALL (IFP) FORMS.
The IFP helps foster the sport's worldwide growth.

2009

THE FIRST USA PICKLEBALL NATIONAL CHAMPIONSHIPS TAKES PLACE.
Nearly four hundred players attend the tournament in Buckeye, Arizona.

There are a lot of roller coasters when you look back at pickleball, historically. It's like, "Wow, I can't believe we made it."

—Jennifer Lucore, professional player, author, and historian

1

HOW IT BEGAN

Considering pickleball's massive rise over the last few years, you could be forgiven for thinking that the sport only recently appeared in our culture. But in reality, pickleball has been around since the 1960s—1965, to be precise.

It all started on Bainbridge Island,[1] a small island in Washington State connected to Seattle by ferry. An affluent, quiet area, Bainbridge—known to locals as "The Rock"—was best known in that era as a key wartime location and the birthplace of a few mildly successful writers (later, it would become something of a haven for authors, with heavyweights like *Captain Underpants* creator Dav Pilkey and *The Nightingale* scribe Kristin Hannah residing on the island). But in the

1960s, it was home to Joel Pritchard, a former army-sergeant-turned-politician after he was elected in 1958 to the Washington House of Representatives. When he wasn't representing his district, Pritchard was known for enjoying a good round of athletics, playing golf and badminton, among other sports. As legend has it, it was on a Saturday in the summertime of 1965 when the congressman returned to his vacation cottage on the island from a golf game along with a friend, businessman Bill Bell, and came up with the idea for pickleball.

When they arrived back home after their round of golf, the two men found their families, including Pritchard's teenage son, Frank, feeling bored and irritated at the lack of activities available to entertain themselves.

"I was bitching to my dad that there was nothing to do on Bainbridge," Frank Pritchard recalled in a 2021 interview with *Pickleball Magazine*.[2] In response, the elder Pritchard told his son that when *he* was a kid, he and his friends would invent games of their own, to which thirteen-year-old Frank replied, "Oh, really? Then why don't you go make up a game?"

Happy to rise to the challenge, Pritchard and Bell first considered starting a routine badminton game, as there was a court on the property, but they couldn't find enough rackets for everyone. Improvising, they grabbed a few Ping-Pong paddles and a perforated

Wiffle ball, and began volleying over the badminton-height (sixty-inch) net, along with their kids. Quickly, the men discovered just how well the plastic ball bounced on the asphalt, and they soon made some adjustments to account for the ball's speed and arc, including lowering the net to a more appropriate height of thirty-six inches. By the end of the weekend, they were hooked—and they knew they needed to share their invention with others as soon as possible.

So, one weekend later, they invited another friend and neighbor, Barney McCallum, the owner of an envelope and printing company, to join them in playing a few rounds. Together the three men decided rules for their new venture, taking inspiration from badminton, Ping-Pong, and tennis. McCallum, who knew his way around tools and construction, helped lead the charge in creating new, better-quality paddles, as the ones Pritchard and Bell had been using had broken easily. A few days later, the trio had created the rudimentary beginnings of a legitimate family-friendly sport—now all it needed was a name.

ABOUT THAT NAME . . .

The first thing most people unfamiliar with the game say when they hear what it's called tends to be some version of "Why *pickle*ball?" And for good reason! Other than the green hues often used on the court, there's nothing about the way the game is set up or the equipment used that has anything to do with the sour-tasting snack. The real reason pickleball got its name isn't related to food at all, but either a boat or a dog—depending on whose story you choose to believe.

Yes, that's right; despite pickleball being as easygoing an activity as it gets, there's some pretty intense disagreement regarding the inspiration for its name. While many fans believe it was inspired by the Pritchard family dog named Pickles, others are adamant that it came instead from a term used in another sport: rowing. In that 2021 *Pickleball Magazine* feature on the sport's origins, the publication researched the two conflicting stories and concluded that the moniker was indeed drawn from the pickle boat of rowing, a.k.a. a crew made up of random, available racers (not to be confused with the pickle boat of sailing, which refers to the final boat to finish a race).[3] The Pritchard family has backed up the theory over the years, with Frank telling the magazine that his mother, Joan, had come up with the idea because pickleball "threw bits of other games into the mix (badminton, table tennis, Wiffle ball)," just like a crew team "threw the leftover non-starter oarsmen into these particular pickle boats." Joan herself also gave support to the story, writing in a 2008 column[4] for her local newspaper that she'd given the game its name because "it reminded me of the Pickle Boat in crew," and dismissing the dog idea by claiming that Pickles was born several years after that 1965 weekend.

It would all make perfect sense—except for the fact that most of the *other* people who witnessed pickleball's formation say that's not even close to what happened. When I reached out to Jennifer Lucore, a professional player and coauthor of the 2018 book *History of Pickleball: More Than 50 Years of Fun!*, to get her take on the debate given her expertise, she jumped at the opportunity to correct what she sees as a major misconception. Over a Zoom call, Lucore told me that before McCallum passed away in 2019, she interviewed him multiple times about pickleball's origin, and the founder swore to her that everyone but the Pritchard family would attest it was Pickles the pup, not boats, who inspired the sport's name.

"He would say all day long, 'yes, it was the dog,'" Lucore said. "He didn't understand why Joan would say something else."

Interviews[5] in 2015 with other early pickleball players for the Pickleball Channel also raised doubts on the pickle boat story. Dick Brown, a friend of the three families who was there for much of the game's initial development, told the channel that it was indeed Joan Pritchard who was responsible for the name, but that she came up with it after watching Pickles run around the family cabin playing with a ball.

According to Brown, Joan said, "'Why don't you name the game pickleball, after Pickles?' And it just hit us. We all thought it was a great name."

If that's true, then why would Joan have spread the pickle boat rumor? According to the people who spoke to the channel, it was likely because of her particular sense of humor, with the interviewees stating a variation of, "If you knew Joan, she was kind of a jokester and that's what she would say," per Lucore.

Alas, with the three founders no longer living and the rest of those originally present in fierce disagreement, we'll never know for sure how, exactly, pickleball got its name. "All these people are this one party, and they all have a different takeaway," said Lucore, shaking her head. "Can't we all agree what we had for dinner? No! And that's what makes it so interesting."

At the end of the day, the historian added, it doesn't really matter. "I love the dog story, but let's just go play," she said with a big laugh.

SPREADING THE WORD

After receiving a name (however it actually happened), pickleball caught on fast on Bainbridge Island, with the families spending the next several months espousing its merits to their friends and neighbors. All the while,

Pritchard, Bell, and McCallum continued to adjust the game's rules and procedures, finalizing details like the correct type of plastic ball, the length of the no-volley zone, and the creation of the double bounce rule. Thanks to those changes, which ensured no player could dominate the game based on height or size alone, pickleball slowly turned into one of the sports world's most unique, and equitable, offerings.

By 1967, word of mouth had led pickleball to be the talk of the town across the island, with McCallum even beginning a business crafting plywood paddles[6] in his garage for eager new players. That year, one of the Pritchards' neighbors, Bob O'Brien, constructed a court in his backyard—the first-ever permanent pickleball court in the world.

It wasn't until a few years later, though, that pickleball *really* took off, thanks to McCallum deciding to bring the game off "The Rock" back to his home in Seattle. There, in the town of Magnolia Bluff, he and his neighbors built new courts to continue spreading the word of the game. To capitalize on the attention, McCallum even began selling pickleball starter sets at trade shows around Washington, aimed largely at school staff members who would hopefully add the game into their curriculum. "They'd put up their little booth, and they'd sell a couple paddles, and the PE teachers would come by with their clipboards," said Lucore.

Business wasn't always smooth; not infrequently, Lucore said, the trade shows wouldn't result in any orders, leading McCallum and his fellow pickleball supporters to worry that the game's popularity was dying off. "They'd come back and be like, 'We're done, right? Nobody wants it,'" Lucore said. "There were so many times that the sport almost didn't make it."

Thankfully, a handful of well-timed orders and media attention helped the players regain confidence in the game's longevity, and McCallum deciding to teach pickleball at schools around Seattle alongside his son also significantly aided its growth. Before long, school districts across the city had adopted the game—and soon, so did schools around all of Washington, plus Oregon, Idaho, Missouri, Texas, Illinois, California, and more.

With such easy access to pickleball, many children growing up in these states at the time didn't realize how small a sport it was compared to most others. Everyone, they assumed, played matches during gym class and had courts in their backyards.

But in actuality, pickleball was still very much a regional game, although its founders were working hard to spread the word as fast as they could. When Pritchard—then a Washington State senator—ran for a seat in the U.S. House of Representatives in the early 1970s, he set up pickleball games at his political fundraisers to entertain the guests. Between his and

McCallum's efforts, it wasn't long before pickleball had started to become a nationally known pastime, with growing interest from potential players and the media. In 1972, the sport's first corporation, Pickle-Ball Inc., was formed; today, fifty years later, the company still sells paddles, nets, and balls to players around the world.

GROWING THE GAME

In the mid-1970s, two major media outlets helped spread news of pickleball even further. First, in 1975, the *National Observer* ran an article[7] explaining the origins of the game and noting its accessibility, writing: "What sports needs is a great leveler, a game in which victory doesn't favor the player who is fastest, tallest, brawniest, youngest or even the most athletic. Stifle the snickering. Pickleball isn't funny. It's fun." (The story also noted that the "proper" pickleball uniform for women consisted of an "orange body suit, puffy polka-dot hat, and dark glasses." That was the seventies for you!)

Soon after, *Tennis* magazine followed up with a piece dubbing pickleball "America's newest racquet sport." Both stories garnered major attention to the game, and so it's no surprise that by the spring of 1976, hype was so high that the first-ever official pickleball tournament was held. Fittingly, the tournament took place in Washington State, at the South Center Athletic Club in the city of Tukwila. More than sixty players competed for the top prizes, including Steve Paranto, a tennis player who'd begun playing the sport at his community college not long before. As Paranto recalled in a 2015 interview with Pickleball Central,[8] none of the players were professionals—in fact, most of them had only started playing pickleball quite recently. "Either they were tennis players that learned at their community college or high school or they were guys who worked at Weyerhaeuser, the company, because they had a private indoor court and they played every day at lunch time," Paranto recounted. "And that was pretty much all the participants in that 'World's First Tournament.'"

Pritchard himself kicked off the competition, which consisted of long, singles matches on a carpet-covered court. After several games (the rules were that players had to win three out of five matches, not two out of three like would be the official pickleball protocol going forward) Paranto's partner, Dave Lester, won first place—making Paranto, as he later told Pickleball Central, "the 'World's First Loser' of pickleball."

In the years following that inaugural tournament, word of the game continued to spread across America, with an increasing number of magazines and newspapers including pickleball coverage alongside tennis or racquetball news. In pickleball's home state of Washington, especially, the game morphed into a bona fide frenzy, with one man, an air force veteran and sports enthusiast named Sid Williams, taking it upon himself to host and organize several more tournaments (with proceeds going to food banks). In March 1984, Williams founded the United States Amateur Pickleball Association (USAPA),[9] naming himself its president and executive director; its goal, then and now, was to "perpetuate the growth and advancement of pickleball on a national level." Soon after its founding, the organization got to work doing just that, developing a pickleball rule book, ranking system, quarterly newsletter, and more.

During the mid to late 1980s, several other changes contributed to pickleball's ongoing rise, including the invention of the first composite paddle, by Boeing industrial engineer Arlen Paranto (Steve's father), in 1984. Working with materials typically used by commercial airlines for planes' floors and structural systems, Paranto fashioned approximately one thousand lightweight paddles through his newly formed company, Pro-lite. The success of these prototypes led to many, many more, and although Paranto eventually sold the company in the mid-1990s, the ingenuity of his tech became the foundation for dozens more paddle manufacturers around the world.

By 1990, there were thousands of players in all fifty states, as well as a few small pickleball championships for serious players. Lucore recalled how her parents, early adopters of the game, would travel in their RV from their home of San Diego to competitions across the country, joined by other older "snowbirds" who enjoyed the prospect of exploring America in the name of pickleball. The more these seniors traveled and shared their love of the game (including with their kids and grandchildren, who shared it with their peers, and so on), the more that players of all ages began to understand the hype.

As a result, the game's popularity continued to rise over the course of the decade, though with few major breakthroughs—save for the 1999 launch of the first pickleball website, Pickleball Stuff (which, remarkably, still exists, albeit in a format so amusingly quaint that navigating through its pages requires a not-insubstantial amount of patience).

Things stayed status quo for pickleball, at least until the start of the new millennium. That's when everything began to change.

A NEW DECADE FOR PICKLEBALL

During the 1980s and '90s, the vast majority of pickleball competitions were held in Washington, and none of them featured more than a few dozen players.

In 2001, however, a tournament at the Happy Trails RV resort in Surprise, Arizona, hosted one hundred players, making it the largest pickleball event ever played. More popular tournaments soon followed in other states, from California to Florida.

Then, in 2003, pickleball was included in the Huntsman World Senior Games, the largest international annual multisports competition for athletes over fifty. That year, around sixty-five pickleball players participated in a few short competitions; in 2021, there would be more than 1,100 players and a full week's worth of events.

Two thousand three also marked thirty-nine known official places to play pickleball throughout the United States and Canada, in addition to at least 150 personal courts. Two years later, in 2005, the USAPA established a new, nonprofit corporation under the name USA Pickleball Association. With a new board of directors overseeing the sport's rules and tournaments, along with a continuously updated database of places to play on its website, the organization's rebranding played a major role in legitimizing pickleball across North America.

Over the next three years, the USA Pickleball database expanded to include 420 official places to play, with pickleball's growing popularity credited in part to a 2008 ABC *Good Morning America* segment on the game—its first-ever mass-media exposure. That same year, pickleball was introduced for the first time to the National Senior Games Association, and a new, revised rule book was published by the governing body.

By the end of the decade, the world of pickleball would see the formation of an international federation (the IFP), a grant program to create many more new courts, and the first-ever all-ages USA Pickleball National Championships tournament, held in Buckeye, Arizona, and featuring nearly four hundred players.

A WORLDWIDE PHENOMENON

Pickleball grew exponentially over the next several years, with the sport boasting more than 2 million players worldwide in 2015, per a report by the SFIA.[10] A year later, the first U.S. Open Pickleball Championships took place, in Naples, Florida, started by Chris Evon and Terri Graham, such avid fans of the game that they quit their jobs in order to organize the competition. Curious why the duo was willing to take such a leap to start a tournament with no guarantee of success, I reached out to Graham. When we spoke on the phone a few days later, she told me that it was because she and Evon both felt deeply at the time that pickleball "needed a big event to really bring it to the next level." While existing tournaments focused solely on the competition aspect, the U.S. Open, they decided, would feature five days' worth of vendors, activities, and opportunities for players and fans to mix between matches. If one thousand players came, Graham and Evon would have counted that first year as a success.

They didn't quite make it to their goal; only 854 players signed on. They did, however, get nearly eight thousand spectators, who'd heard about the chance to watch pickleball while hanging with other fans in Florida and made a vacation out of the trip. "The cars just kept coming and coming," Graham remembered, the awe in her voice still evident all these years later.

In 2017, USA Pickleball and the International Pickleball Teaching Professional Association (IPTPA) teamed up to launch the Pickleball Hall of Fame,[11] whose aim, per its website, is to recognize "individuals who have achieved exceptional results in pickleball play over the course of their career, as well as those who have made exceptional contributions to the growth, development and leadership of the game." Its inaugural inductees included Pritchard, McCallum, and Williams, among others, and their photos were displayed at a temporary museum in Kent, Washington (a permanent location, in Austin, Texas, is in the works).

Over the next year, the pickleball community saw more highlights, including the moving of the National Championships from Arizona to Indian Wells, California, home to the second-largest outdoor tennis stadium in the world. Being able to showcase pickleball on such a major, renowned stage was a watershed moment for the sport. Featuring a $75,000 cash prize—then the biggest in the sport's history—the 2018 tournament saw more than 2,200 players and many more spectators, including none other than a ninety-two-year-old Barney McCallum himself.

Justin Maloof, the chief operating officer of USA Pickleball and one of the people who helped organize McCallum's visit to Indian Wells, told me over a phone call that he remembered the founder seeming awed by the scope of the championships. "It actually brought tears to his eyes," Maloof recalled. "Here was a guy who was there back in '65 when they invented this thing, and for him to see it reach, in essence, the pinnacle of the sport at the time . . . he was just overwhelmed by it."

More changes were to come shortly after. Around late 2018, the game's top players began calling themselves professional athletes, and a select few even had sponsors, but there was little in the way of backing from larger pickleball organizations. Enter the Professional Pickleball Association (PPA) and the Association of Pickleball Professionals (APP), now the sport's two major tours, with dozens of professional tournaments throughout the world.

"We saw the opportunity to come in and really formalize what was going on," said Connor Pardoe, the

PPA's commissioner and founder. "We took a couple of the bigger tournaments out there, purchased one, partnered with another, and created twelve events of our own and went for it."

According to Pardoe, the fact that the APP's founders clearly thought the same thing—both organizations announced their launches within two weeks of each other—only served to emphasize the need for a proper pickleball tour with organized, highly attended competitions.

That first year, the PPA Tour stops were fairly low-key, with midsize venues, minimal prize money, and few full-time employees running the show. "It was more of a ma-and-pa operation to now, where it's a lot more of a corporate structure," recalled Pardoe.

Thanks to funding from sponsors and increased attention to the sport, though, the next year's tour—along with the APP competitions and other, nonsanctioned pickleball events—had far more to offer. By the end of 2019, pickleball was so popular that it'd been deemed one of the fastest-growing sports in America, per the SFIA, with no sign of slowing down. It marked a triumphant win for the once-tiny game, if also, perhaps, the limits on just how far it could truly go. After all, as popular as pickleball had become and as fun as it was to play, even its biggest fans didn't dare dream that it could ever get as massive as, say, tennis or golf. But then, 2020 came around and created a landscape perfectly primed for a sport like pickleball to thrive.

THE PANDEMIC CHANGES EVERYTHING

In February 2020, the PPA held the Foot Solutions Arizona Grand Slam in the city of Mesa, attracting the largest number of pickleball players an Arizona tournament had ever seen, including pros like Ben Johns and Kyle Yates, and a substantial prize pot for winners. Yet in the grand scheme of the sport, the competition wouldn't have been particularly notable— save for the fact that it was the last major pickleball event to occur before the COVID-19 pandemic took hold in America.

Looking back, Pardoe told me, it's hard to understate the impact of the Grand Slam—which gave thousands of new fans a glimpse at the sport's growing popularity and potential—not being canceled.

"If that tournament didn't happen, I think you're looking at a whole different world of the pickleball landscape," he explained. "It would've been a long time without events, and I don't know how motivated people would've continued to be."

Without the hype from the tournament, many people might have lost interest in the sport, and even Pardoe and the PPA might have had to turn their attentions elsewhere. But because the Grand Slam successfully went on, Pardoe said, "we saw what pickleball could be before the pandemic hit."

Indeed, when the crisis took hold a month later, pickleball wasn't one of its many casualties. As countless people adjusted to their difficult new reality, many of them—like me—looked to the sport as a way to stay active and entertained, often from the comfort of their own homes. They built courts out of tape on their driveway or converted tennis courts to pickleball; they teamed up with family members for impromptu games or headed to their local gyms or community centers to find new opponents. Many discovered pickleball for the very first time, or used their longtime skills to teach the game to new fans. They were young and old, male and female, casual players and serious athletes. Together they turned pickleball into an even bigger sensation than anyone could have imagined.

"A lot of pickleball companies that are sponsors for our tour sold out of pickleball equipment during the pandemic," said Hannah Johns, the head of content for the PPA. "Since then, we've just seen such an explosion."

I can see the impact clearly right in my home of Raleigh, North Carolina, where pickleball has thrived over the past few years. On any given day, the city's twelve permanent outdoor courts,[12] several dozen indoor courts, and who knows how many home courts are full of players dinking, serving, and volleying to their hearts' content. Even my local pool club, which barely fits a hundred people on its property, is home to a pickleball court (where I play, of course, alongside Kurt and a few of our neighbor friends).

Pickleball is growing fast here, and everywhere else. All across the country, cities and towns are racing to accommodate the fast-rising number of players. In Avalon, New Jersey, a resort area home to pickleball's Avalon Open tournament each May, the game is so popular that in the summer of 2021, there was a shortage of courts available for both locals and tourists alike. As such, pickleball ambassadors (a.k.a. volunteer representatives of the sport) have been working around the clock with the town's leaders to keep up with demand and prevent the issue from happening again.

Even in many bigger cities, interest in pickleball is so high that there are often wait times for fans looking to get in some playing time. At the Goldman Tennis Center in San Francisco, for instance, the tennis courts were booked just 58 percent of the time during a three-month period in 2021, according to the *San Francisco Chronicle*. The pickleball courts, though? They were booked a whopping 95 percent of the time.[13]

The professional side of the sport is also working overtime to keep up with the growth. The average stop on the PPA's tour now gets more than 1,000 players and five times that many fans; over the course of 2022, the organization predicts that more than 30,000 players will participate in PPA events—and that's not counting the 275,000 pickleball fans who will tune in via networks like ESPN, the Tennis Channel, or the more recently created, online-only Pickleball Channel to watch the tournaments from home.

"Even as recent as a year or two ago, people were telling us, 'Pickleball is not a spectator sport, you're never gonna get people to watch pros and care or have it broadcast on a major network. It's never gonna happen, it's just not what the sport is—it's social, it's fun, it's friendly, but it's not competitive like that,'" said Johns.

As it turns out, though, watching players dive across the court for a return and hit seemingly impossible shots from the baseline—often with commentary from pickleball's top players—does make for quality entertainment. With so much love from viewers, Johns said, "I can proudly say we've proved them wrong."

More businesses, too, are getting involved, sponsoring top players like Ben Johns and Simone Jardim and providing the funding needed to take tournaments to the next level. At this rate, it may not be long before pickleball overtakes some of its legendary competitors—tennis, racquetball, even Ping-Pong—in terms of worldwide popularity. And while you can certainly credit the game's ease of play, unique nature, and accessibility for its ascent, it's the players—people like me and you—who have made the biggest difference in pickleball's incredible journey. By playing the sport and sharing our love for it with others, we've helped transform pickleball from a quirky, little-known activity to a bona fide phenomenon adored by millions of people around the globe. So let's keep spreading the word and helping pickleball grow, because the more people who play, the better it is for us all.

Tracie Holmes, the player, ambassador, and coach from New Jersey, told me that when she first got into the game, she didn't expect to ever teach it to anyone else. Yet when her town's representatives asked her one summer if she would provide lessons to beginners, she hesitantly said yes—and was shocked by how rewarding it felt to see her students get immersed in the pickleball world. Years later, she still coaches new players every summer, and plans to volunteer her services as long as there's interest.

"I've had people come up to me and say, 'Oh, you're the person that taught me how to play—thank you so much for introducing me to this sport,'" said Holmes. "That was really meaningful to me."

Being able to bring new people into the game is Holmes's favorite part of being involved in pickleball because, she explained, "You know you've had a positive impact on people and were able to introduce them to something that they may end up loving as much as you do."

My friends and I learned how to play at our local community center, and the four of us just had a blast. We had no clue what we were doing, but that's what's great about pickleball—you can learn it pretty quickly, so by the end of the two-hour period, we were playing some fun games, having a great time, and getting exercise. . . . And once I learned how to play, it kind of clicked, like, "Oh, this is incredible."

—Laura Gainor, USA Pickleball marketing consultant and founder of Pickleball in the Sun

2

PICKLEBALL 101

I f you're reading this book, there's a fair chance
that you've partaken in a game or two (or perhaps
many) of pickleball before. But even frequent
players can use a reminder of the basics every now and
then—and if you're one of the lucky few who've *never*
played pickleball before and are considering giving
it a try, then consider this chapter your abbreviated
guide to understanding the game (you can find more
detailed explanations of the rules in the 2022 USA
Pickleball/IFP Rulebook, downloadable online).

THE BASICS

The first thing to know about pickleball is what it's
not—not tennis, not racquetball, not Ping-Pong, not

paddleball, and not badminton. Yes, it's true that the sport incorporates aspects of each of those sports, and as you read in the previous chapter, its creators were indeed inspired by several of those existing games when brainstorming their new invention. Yet pickleball is 100 percent its own, original entity, with rules and techniques not seen in any other sport—and that's what makes it so much fun.

At its core, pickleball is a paddle sport in which two teams of players—singles or doubles—send a plastic ball back and forth over a net until one side wins.[1] It's played on a small, badminton-sized court, and players serve the ball diagonally and underhand. The ball must bounce once before a volley can start, and there's a seven-foot no-volley zone on each side of the net, called the "Kitchen," to prevent any spiking. Only the serving team can score points, and the first side to earn 11 points by a margin of at least two wins the game.

If it sounds simple, it should—pickleball really is one of the easiest sports there is to learn, which is a main reason for its massive popularity (becoming great, of course, takes far more effort). Kids and adults alike can just pick up a paddle and start playing after a quick tutorial, and even those who decide to go in totally blind usually only need a few hours on the court to get the hang of things.

That said, there is much more to the game than just its most fundamental summary. To start, let's break down some of the most common pickleball terms all players should know. (If you're a tennis player, you'll probably recognize a few of these!)

FIFTEEN MUST-KNOW PICKLEBALL TERMS

ACE—A serve that isn't returned by your opponent.

BACKSPIN—Striking the ball with high-to-low motion, causing it to spin in the opposite direction of its path. You might also hear this type of shot referred to as a "chop" or "slice."

DINK—A shot that arcs over the net and lands in your opponents' non-volley zone. (Unsurprisingly given the fun-sounding word, there's no shortage of pickleball merch sporting sayings like "I dink therefore I am" or "Dink then drink.")

DRIVE—A straight and low shot that lands deep in your opponents' backcourt.

DROP SHOT—A shot that clears the net and lands in front of your opponents.

GROUND STROKE—A ball that's hit after one bounce.

JUNIOR—A pickleball player between the ages of seven and nineteen.

KITCHEN—The seven-foot non-volley zone in front of the net on both sides.

LET—A serve that hits the net, landing in the service court.

LOB—A shot that sends the ball up high and lands deep.

OVERHEAD SMASH—A powerful, overhand shot aimed downward into your opponents' court (often as a return to a high shot).

POACH—To cross over to your partner's side of the court and steal a shot.

RALLY—Game play that starts from the time the ball is served and ends when there's a fault.

SIDE OUT—When one team loses the serve, giving the opponents the chance to serve.

TOPSPIN—Putting spin on the ball from low to high, therefore causing it to spin in the same direction as it flies.

These are just a handful of the many pickleball-related terms out there, of course. For a full list, check out the glossary of definitions at the back of this book.

Now let's dive into some specific pickleball components, beginning with one of the most important of them all: the serve.

THE SERVE

The pickleball serve[2] is notable for two unique things: its diagonal aim and underhand motion. Standing in the right-hand back square of the court, the server must move their arm upward to strike the ball with the paddle below their waist level, and at least one foot must be on the playing surface behind the back line. They can serve in a forehand or backhand motion, but bouncing the ball isn't allowed—the server must hit the ball in the air, and most importantly, it must fully clear the non-volley zone (the aforementioned Kitchen) before landing in their opponents' diagonal service court. If it doesn't, or if it hits the non-volley zone line, then it's considered out.

When a point is scored, the server switches sides and sends the next serve from the left side of the court, and continues to switch back and forth as more points are scored until committing a fault. (In a game of singles, the server serves from the right-side court when the score is even but from the left side when the score is odd). Only one serve attempt is allowed, with one exception: in the rare case when the ball touches the net on the serve but still lands in the correct service court, the server may get another shot.

At the start of a new game, the first team to serve must give up the ball to their opponents after the first serving fault. However, after that, both members of the team (assuming it's a game of doubles) get the chance to serve and fault before having to turn over the ball. When a team *does* win a serve, it's always the player in the right-hand side of the court who starts play.

As for which team gets to serve first at the very start of the game? That can be determined however you like—coin flip, rock-paper-scissors, etc. As long as the method is deemed fair by all, then it's allowed.

THE KITCHEN

The Kitchen refers to the seven-feet zone on either side of the net where volleying is prohibited. It prevents players from smashing the ball over the net, thereby extending the length of each game and making it a fairer playing field for all. If a player steps into that zone (or on the line) to volley the ball, it's considered a fault, but they're allowed to be in the zone at any other time during the game.

As for where the name came from, no one's totally sure, but the main theory is that it was inspired by shuffleboard,[3] because in that game, the "kitchen" refers to the area behind the main scoring zones where, when landed in, costs a player ten points.

THE TWO-BOUNCE RULE

Another crucial element of pickleball is the two-bounce rule, also referred to as the double-bounce rule. This says that after the ball is served, the receiving team must let it bounce once before returning—and then the *serving* team also must let it bounce before sending it back. Once the ball has bounced in each team's court, then the teams can either volley the ball (a.k.a. hit it before it bounces again) or play it off the bounce (otherwise known as a ground stroke).

VOLLEYING

As players of tennis or volleyball know well, a volley is defined as a ball being hit in the air without bouncing first. During a pickleball game, a player can volley only if they place both feet behind the Kitchen line— otherwise, it's considered a fault.

FAULTS

In pickleball (and many other sports), a fault is any action that violates a rule of the game and causes play to be stopped. You might know it as a "dead ball," but whatever you want to call it, it means the same thing.

Stepping into the Kitchen to volley counts as a fault, as said, as does:

- Serving the ball or returning a serve without the ball bouncing first
- Hitting the ball not into your opponents' diagonal service court
- Hitting the ball into the net

- Hitting the ball *under* the net, or between the net and the net post
- Touching the net with your body or paddle
- Hitting a ball that landed out of bounds or on your own side of the court
- Failing to return the ball before it bounces twice
- Stopping a live ball while it's still valid (that is, catching it midair)

If the serving team gets a fault, they lose the serve, but if the receiving team gets a fault, it gives a point to their opponents.

SCORING

I'm not going to lie—pickleball scoring is . . . complicated. Unlike in most sports, where the score is read aloud as two numbers, pickleball requires players to call out *three* numbers before each new serve: the server score, receiver score, and the server number. For example, in a game in which Team A has four points and Team B has six, and Team A's second player is serving, the score would be announced as 4-6-2. Take note, though, that the server number only applies to that specific turn, as when the serving team's score is an even number, the player who was the first server stands in the right-side court to serve or receive, but if the score is an odd number, they'll go to the left-side court, instead.

If that all sounds confusing, you're not alone. It's all too common for pickleball players to lose track of which number server they are, since they simultaneously have to remember each side's points and state them in the correct order. Even professional pickleball athletes aren't the biggest fans of the way the game is scored—and not just because of the three numbers needed, but the lack of time typically given to players in fast-moving games to figure them out.

"If I'm having a rally that is 160 shots long, by the time the point is done, I'm tired and I don't even know where I am. And the problem is, I only have five seconds before the ref is ready to call the score and get the next point going," said Jessie Irvine, one of the top five-ranked women's pickleball players in the world. Often in tournaments, Irvine added, she'll find herself asking the referee to confirm the score and server number, a process that can be frustrating for both her and her opponents. "There are a lot of players that don't like that you can ask these questions because they're like, 'Well you should know, you shouldn't be able to ask all these things,'" she noted. "But you don't want to serve from the wrong spot, and you don't want to receive from the right spot."

ADAPTIVE RULES

While pickleball has always attracted many players with disabilities due to its small court and generally inclusive feel (in addition to its many other merits), it was only seven years ago that a chapter was added to the official rule book to account for the specific needs of wheelchair pickleball. The full list can be viewed online, but some notable changes, created by USA Pickleball in collaboration with wheelchair pickleball players, are below:[4]

- Half-court for Singles—If both players are in wheelchairs, the game can be played entirely on half-court, and both server and receiver can serve, receive, and play a point from their service and receiving court.
- Two-Bounce Rule—A wheelchair pickleball player is allowed to bounce the ball twice on their side of the net before returning, rather than once.
- Service—The player should be in a stationary position and then is allowed one push before hitting the ball.
- Non-Volley Zone—If a wheelchair player hits a ball into the zone during a volley, it counts as a fault only if their larger-rear wheels are in

the zone, too. And *after* hitting a bounced ball, their larger-rear wheels have to get outside the zone's boundaries before returning the volley.

In games where the players are of mixed ability—that is, a wheelchair player and standing player working as a team or as opponents—then they each abide by their own appropriate rules. That form of playing, a.k.a. hybrid pickleball, is increasingly common as more players of all abilities get word of the sport.

Of course, playing pickleball in a wheelchair has its challenges, especially for people not previously familiar with the world of adaptive sports. When I posted in a popular Facebook group for pickleball fans, I came across Jamie Elliott, an ambassador and retired stuntwoman (she's worked on *Robocop* and *Born on the Fourth of July,* among other films) who was paralyzed from the waist down in 2019 after surgery to remove a tumor on her spine. An avid pickleball fan who first discovered the sport way back in 1990, the Angel Fire, New Mexico–based athlete had played most weekdays prior to getting sick, even traveling frequently to compete at high-level tournaments like the National Senior Games Association. When multiple cancerous tumors forced her to spend twenty-two months off the courts in recovery, Elliott turned to other, more easily adaptable sports like swimming, but nothing filled the void. "I missed pickleball so much," she told me.

Desperate for a way to get back into the game, Elliott reached out to Pamela Fontaine, a medal-winning Paralympic athlete in basketball and table tennis who also plays pickleball. Fontaine's encouragement, plus a successful Google search for "wheelchair pickleball," gave Elliott hope that her pickleball-playing days weren't behind her.

In January 2021, she purchased a sports wheelchair and promptly named it Barney after McCallum, one of the game's founders. Then she spent considerable time adjusting to the various intricacies of playing para-pickleball. "It was a whole new learning experience," she recalled. "My body was lower from sitting, so I had to learn when and what height I could take any overhead shot. Turning my chair, to give me more room to take a shot so I didn't hit my wheels. Moving to get out of the way of an oncoming ball."

Elliott also had to regularly remind her partners and opponents about the game's adaptations for players like herself, such as the two-bounce rule. But before too long, she had become such a natural at para-pickleball that she started reentering tournaments, playing both hybrid and wheelchair doubles. When we e-mailed, she sent me photos of herself competing, and it was clear from the expressions on her face just how glad she was to be back on the court with her trusty chair.

"I've read stories about how pickleball has saved someone's life," Elliott said. "Barney saved my life."

PICKLEBALL'S GOLDEN RULE

Brushing up on your terminology and learning the game's various forms are both important, but they aren't the only essentials for becoming a real pickleball player. You also need to understand pickleball protocol, a.k.a. the Golden Rule.

As a game that was originally invented by three fathers to play with their families, pickleball has always been about more than just competition and athletics. Participants are expected to be true team players, prioritizing fairness and cooperation over simply winning a point. This goes for the actual rules of the game, in that either partner during a doubles match is allowed to make calls, and no point, whether it's the first of the game or the match point, is worth more than another. But the idea also goes for the behavior between players.

"Pickleball is a game that requires cooperation and courtesy," says the official USA Pickleball/IFP

Rulebook.[5] "A sense of fair play from giving the opponent the benefit of any doubt is essential in maintaining the game's underlying principles of fun and competition."

When Cynthia Etheridge, a player, entrepreneur, marketing director, and musician from my home of Raleigh, teaches beginners the rules of the game, she also makes sure to instill in them those bigger pickleball values. First and foremost, she explains to them, you should introduce yourself to your opponents, creating a friendly, personal relationship that lasts through the game. Then you play fairly and respectfully, and when things come to a close, you acknowledge each other's efforts—win or lose.

"At the end of the game, no matter who you are, you all come together and you tap your paddles and you say, 'Good game,'" Etheridge said, adding that it's an extremely rare sight to see a player angrily walk off the court after a loss: "You just don't do that in pickleball."

Curious if this attitude was equally common in top-level pickleball, I asked several pros about their experiences with sportsmanship on the court. Zane Navratil, the number-two-rated men's singles player worldwide, revealed that in professional pickleball, players take that Golden Rule extremely seriously—perhaps even more so than amateurs.

"You don't have those adversarial matches quite as much as you might in other sports," he explained when we spoke over a Zoom call. "Because if I make a bad line call, I know I have to look you in the eye next week, or the rest of this week—I could play you on Friday and have to play you on Saturday and Sunday, twice each day."

And "because it's such a small community," Navratil continued, "word gets around quickly" about "who's an a-hole, and who plays fair and is a nice person."

Thankfully, the vast majority of pickleball fans at all levels fall into the latter category, respectful of their fellow players and more than happy to share their love of the game with anyone who asks. It's that attitude that makes pickleball so special, and a game anyone can feel comfortable playing—and winning.

You've got all your Wilsons and your Franklins getting into pickleball and making paddles and balls, selling equipment and clothing, the whole gamut . . . it's become a multimillion-dollar industry.

—David Jordan, director for pickleball at the Huntsman World Senior Games and former president of USA Pickleball

3

COURTS AND EQUIPMENT

When Kurt and I were first gifted those pickleball paddles back in April 2020, we knew we wanted to set up a game ASAP to try it out. As two newcomers to the sport, though, we didn't have a clue how one went about finding a pickleball court, let alone during a point in the pandemic when simply venturing out of the house was a major risk. So, with the help of Kurt's dad and stepmom, we fashioned our own makeshift court in the driveway of his family's house—and we were thrilled to discover that the process was so easy, it was practically foolproof.

Whether you're also looking to create a driveway court or are converting another space (like a tennis court) into a pickleball haven, here's a rundown of how to make it happen.

BUILDING THE COURT

Pickleball can be played on either concrete or asphalt, so driveways and side streets are both fine options for casual play. Many people, though, prefer playing pickleball on surfaces already meant for other sports, such as basketball, volleyball, badminton, and, of course, tennis courts. Wherever you decide to set up shop, there are a few technical things that all nonofficial pickleball courts require:

The Right Space. To build (or convert) a pickleball court, the first thing you need to do is determine if it'll fit into the area you have in mind. While the actual playing lines of the court measure out to 20 by 44 feet, you'll need a total space of at least 30 by 60 feet (34 by 64 is ideal). It's also recommended that you pick an area with a north-south orientation, to avoid having the sun shine too intensely in players' eyes.

The Proper Dimensions. In addition to the figuring out the dimensions of the court itself, you'll also need to determine the placement of the net, non-volley zone, and different areas of play. The two service areas (right and left) on each side of the court should be 15 by 10 feet, and should be separated equally down the middle. Those service areas should end at the start of the seven-foot zone in front of the net on each side, a.k.a. the Kitchen. As for the net itself, it should be 36 inches high on the sideline, and 34 at the center (slightly lower than in tennis, so you'll need to adjust the net if you're playing on a tennis court).

Clear Court Markers. If you're playing on a surface that's typically used for another sport or activity (basically, any place that's not an actual pickleball court), you'll want to mark all the playing lines (that is, the baselines, sidelines, non-volley line, non-volley zones, centerlines, and service courts) with a bright, noticeable material. Many people working with temporary courts choose to use tape, and if you go this route, you'll need about two hundred feet (about a full roll) to cover the length of all the court's lines.[1] Chalk is another popular option, but keep in mind that if you're sharing the space with non-pickleball players, they might not be pleased to see lines drawn on the court for days following a game. Paint works, too, but for the same reason, it should only be used on your own property or in a permanent pickleball space. If your court is temporary or shared, you might want to consider vinyl court marker lines, which are made of rubber and come in both straight and corner shapes to give the court a clear, visible outline. They're easy to set up and take down, and they don't leave any markings on the ground.

A Solid Perimeter. Assuming you're playing on a surface that's larger than the exact dimensions for your newly created pickleball court, you'll want to put up a barrier of some sort to keep any missed balls from rolling too far away. After all, no one wants to spend the bulk of their pickleball game sprinting up and down the court in search of wayward balls, right? If you plan to keep the pickleball court set up for years to come, consider building an actual fence, but if the space is just meant to be temporary or frequently converted back and forth, any kind of mock barrier will do.

And that's it! Now, let's talk about the tools you need to actually *use* that court you've just created or converted.

FINDING THE RIGHT EQUIPMENT

In the early days of the game, only a handful of companies carried equipment like paddles and balls, and the few items that *were* available weren't always of the highest quality, or even specific to pickleball (badminton nets, lowered to the floor, were frequent sights on courts). But as interest in the sport increased over the years, more and more retailers got into the game, and today there are more than three hundred manufacturers producing pickleball paddles alone.

With such a surplus of options, though, it's understandable if the idea of shopping for pickleball equipment can feel more overwhelming than exciting. After all, it's not just about deciding between colors or comparing two price points; the right supplies should be suited to your specific playing needs, with everything from the size of your hand to the location of your court taken into consideration.

That's not to say you need to be an expert on the game or know your exact playing style, however, to make smart pickleball purchases. Below, I've broken down each type of equipment needed to play, so you can make your shopping decisions with confidence.

PICKING OUT A PADDLE

Smaller than a tennis racquet but bigger than a Ping-Pong paddle, pickleball paddles are lightweight and easily graspable. While old-school paddles were made from wood, newer versions are typically constructed from aluminum, graphite, and other similar materials, reducing drag and making them more enjoyable for all players to use.

Not every pickleball paddle is alike, however, and there are a few key factors to keep in mind when browsing the options.

Weight. This is the most important priority in choosing a pickleball paddle, as the amount it weighs affects how it will feel in your hand and how you will use it on the court. Pickleball paddles fall into three categories: lightweight (under 7.3 ounces, so about two or three times the weight of a Ping-Pong paddle), midweight (7.3 to 8.4 ounces), and heavy (8.5 to 14 ounces, in range with a tennis racquet's weight).[2]

Lighter paddles are great for increased control over the ball and maneuverability, and reduce stress on the elbow and shoulder, making them ideal for players who suffer from tennis elbow, arthritis, or other similar injuries. Heavier paddles, on the other hand, are all about increased power and ability to hit the ball deep in the court, and they require less effort than lighter paddles to deliver those hits (which often suits tennis players used to hitting hard drives off hefty racquets). Keep in mind, though, that their greater weight means that they'll wear on you faster over the course of a long game, and using a paddle that's too heavy for you can put unnecessary strain on your wrist. Plus, hitting a ball extra hard doesn't necessarily make it travel substantially faster, so it may not even be worth the effort.

If you're not sure what weight is right for you, midsize paddles may be the way to go, and you can always go up or down if you decide your style of play requires a different option. If you're able, stop by a sporting goods store and swing around a few options to determine what feels best. Think of it like finding the right-size bowling ball. You don't know until you try!

Grip. After you've gotten the proper paddle weight sorted out, it's time to think about grip. You want a paddle with a grip circumference that matches your hand size, making it easy to hold; the wrong size grip can disrupt your play and make everything more difficult. "If the handle doesn't fit your hand, then you won't understand the orientation of the paddle after that," said Pat Bernardo, owner of the popular equipment dealer Pickleball Galaxy. A longtime and competitive player himself (we were introduced by one of his frequent opponents, Dave Gould, whom I also interviewed for this book), Bernardo is passionate about getting the right supplies into beginners' hands. Otherwise, he told me, they end up suffering injuries, getting frustrated on the court, and returning equipment after just a few ill-advised uses. All too often, the primary reason is grip.

Usually, Bernardo said, tennis players switching over to pickleball gravitate toward larger grips since they're familiar with holding thicker racquets, while racquetball players used to using their wrists more than their hands are typically comfortable with smaller grips. The smaller the grip, he explained, the easier it will be for you put spin on the ball and gain more control, which can increase your serve power, too. Larger grips, though, are good for keeping your hits

COURTS AND EQUIPMENT

stable and reducing strain on your wrists, elbows, and shoulders.

To measure your grip size, first look at your height. Those under 5'2" usually need a 4" grip, while those between 5'3" and 5'8" will likely want a 4⅛" to 4¼" grip, and those over 5'9" probably require a 4½" grip. To get even more specific, you can use a ruler to measure the distance from the top of your ring finger down to the middle of your palm. That number is the grip size you need.

If you get a paddle and find that it's too narrow a grip for you, don't immediately return it—you can always add a layer of overgrip (also known as overwrap), a soft, clothlike tape used in several sports to wrap around the grip of a paddle or racquet to add extra padding and increase the handle's circumference.

Material. What a pickleball paddle is made from is another major factor to consider when picking a racquet. There are three materials to consider: wood, composite, and graphite. As said, older paddles were typically built with wood, and while they're not as common now, they are still available to buy (as shown by the wood starter set that I began playing with). The main benefit of these paddles is the price— wood paddles are by far the least expensive of all the options, costing as low as $11. The downside, though, is that they're significantly heavier than other types of paddles, so unless wood is the only option available to you, you probably want to consider going for graphite- or composite-made paddles instead.

If you want a paddle that's lighter than wood but is still fairly low-priced, composite is the way to go. These paddles' textured surfaces make them great for giving shots some serious spin, and they tend to range from around $30 to $70. If you can afford to spend a bit more, though, consider picking up a graphite paddle instead, as they promise the lightest yet strongest delivery of all thanks to their double-sided thin graphite faces. These paddles generally start around $50 and can go up to $100 or more.

As for where to buy paddles, there are hundreds of companies that sell them (as well as overgrips), ranging from general retailers like Amazon and Target to pickleball-centric shops like Pickleball Central and Bernardo's Pickleball Galaxy.

CHOOSING A BALL

Okay, so you have a paddle—now you need a ball! Despite pickleball and tennis sharing some similarities, the balls are actually quite different. For one thing, a pickleball ball is made of plastic, and for another, similar to a Wiffle ball, it's covered in tiny circular holes (anywhere between 26 and 40 of them). Also, a pickleball ball is slightly larger than a tennis ball, coming in at just under three inches in diameter. It's a bit lighter, too, making it a perfect match for the lightweight pickleball paddle.

Additionally, unlike tennis balls, which are usually only one color, pickleball balls come in several color options, from green to pink to white. If you're planning on competing in tournaments, the IFP requires that the ball be a single color, but otherwise you're free to use whatever color (or colors) of ball you like. A lot of players go for bright yellows, oranges, and greens for best visibility, but it's really just a matter of taste.

As for the *type* of ball you get, though, that depends on whether you're primarily playing pickleball indoors or outdoors.[3] Indoor pickleballs are softer, lighter, and less bouncy than outdoor balls, and they have larger and fewer holes. These features will give you more control over your shots, and the ball's lightweight feel makes them quieter and less likely to crack than their outdoor counterparts. The negatives, though, are that these balls *will* have a bit more drag and can be harder to slam.[4]

Meanwhile, outdoor balls are harder, bouncier, and a little bit heavier, too, due to the different surfaces they're meant to be used on. You'll have less control with these balls, but your shots will be quicker and more intense, and their heaviness means they'll be less susceptible to wind. Just be prepared to replace your outdoor pickleballs often, because they tend to suffer cracks after frequent play.

Cost-wise, a twelve-pack of either type of pickleball will set you back anywhere between $12–$30, on average, so when choosing a kind of ball to purchase, it should just come down to where you plan to play most often.

NABBING A NET

Let's talk nets. As mentioned earlier, a pickleball net should be 36 inches high on the sides, and 34 inches at the center. But in addition to ensuring that the net you buy has the right dimensions, you want to make sure that it's durable (especially if you're playing outdoors and know it'll be susceptible to the elements) and that it's portable, since you'll likely be taking it apart every so often as needed.[5] Also, don't forget to check to see if the net you're ordering comes with poles and sleeves (many do), or if you need to buy them separately.

Other than that, though, there are no other major must-haves for a pickleball net. It's far more about personal preference, as some players gravitate toward more lightweight models that are easy to set up, while others like heavier-duty ones that feel firmer in place. The tautness of a net is often a sign of its value, said Bernardo, noting, "the better quality net that you get, the less sag that you're gonna have to deal with."

Players looking to save can find a net for around $40 on Amazon or Walmart, while pricier options can cost up to $100 or more.

LIGHTING IT UP

As long as you have the right paddles, balls, and net, plus a good surface to play on, that's really all you need to get a pickleball game going. There are a few additional purchases you can make to take things up a notch, however, starting with lighting.

If you're primarily playing pickleball on a home court, adding some lighting to your setup can make it a truly impressive place to play, especially at night. There are no set requirements for the lighting of an outdoor pickleball court, but most guidelines suggest that players purchase at least two 18-to-26-foot poles and LED fixtures.[6] The poles need to be tall so that players won't lose track of the ball if it goes into a high arc, and the larger the court (or courts), the higher the poles should be. To give the court ample light and avoid creating glare, the poles should be mounted at least two feet back from the center of the court on each side. As for the LEDs themselves, it's suggested that they be around 1,500 watts in order to fully light up the court.

Of course, giving your court professional-level lighting won't come cheap. Most lighting packages cost a pretty penny, with the price range going from $3,000 to $12,000 depending on the number of poles and lights needed. But if you're a pickleball fan who's serious about making the most of your playing time, the investment may just be worth it.

BUYING THE PROPER SHOES

Sure, you can head to the court in regular old sneakers, but many people who play frequently purchase shoes specifically made for the game. You can search by brand and price point, of course, but it's the type of shoe that matters most. Like with balls, there are two distinct types of shoes for indoor and outdoor pickleball, due to the different surfaces.

Indoor pickleball shoes have "a softer rubber sole" to accommodate the sealer used on gym floors and, as such, are similar to racquetball or volleyball shoes, explained Bernardo. Outdoor shoes, meanwhile, feature a harder bottom base that's "more like a traditional tennis shoe."

It's crucial to buy the right pickleball shoes for the surface you're using to avoid disastrous consequences—especially on hot summer days. "If you bring indoor shoes outside, sometimes the temperature alone has a bad effect on the adhesive stuff that they use to bind the bottoms together— that's why a lot of people's bottoms come off," explained Bernardo. "They're playing in one hundred degrees outside, and if they have the wrong shoe, it's melting."

PROTECTING YOUR EYES

The last item to think about picking up, especially if you're a newer player, is eyeguards. I know, I know, it might feel like overkill—is dinking back and forth really that dangerous? But while getting hit in the face by a slow-moving ball may not top your list of concerns, getting hit in the face by a *paddle* should.

"I've seen some devastating hits," remarked Bernardo. "You and your partner are going for the same ball, it's up in the air, you both swing overhead, and somebody gets smacked in the face. I've seen that so many times."

So yes: eyeguards. The good news is, they don't even need to have lenses, which can annoyingly fog up or reflect glare during a game. As long as they have a frame offering your eyes ample protection, then you're good to go.

Once you've gotten all your equipment and set up your court, you'll be just about ready to play!

GROWING
YOUR GAME

Confession: I love pickleball, but I'm not exactly the most impressive player out there. Sure, I know my dinks from my drives, but I'm certainly not an expert, nor am I particularly athletic—just ask my high school softball coach for proof. Plus, my pickleball playing time over the years has been limited to casual games with family and friends, most of whom are at the same low skill level as I am.

Talking to so many talented players while working on this book, though, motivated me to improve my own abilities; after all, nothing is quite as humbling

The first time I gave pickleball lessons, there were some very nonathletic people that came out that really had no hand-eye coordination and couldn't even hit the ball over the net—like very, very beginners. But by the end of even the first session, I saw a significant improvement, and I knew I was introducing them to a new thing that was gonna enhance their lives.

—Tracie Holmes, player, ambassador, and coach

as having to admit to people who literally devote their lives to a sport that you're still learning the basics. So I decided to take my first-ever pickleball lesson, meaning that, first things first, I needed to find a coach.

Like in any other sport, the purpose of a pickleball coach is to help you improve your techniques, learn more key strategies, and feel encouraged to be the best player you can possibly be. That goes for whether you're planning on entering tournaments or just want to beat your friend on a home court, as a good coach should be able to assist you with any of those goals. While some pickleball coaches are current or former pro players themselves (many of the world's best players teach newbies on the side), many more are simply everyday talented players who enjoy helping others develop their own abilities. After all, a person doesn't need to be a top-level competitor in order to be an effective teacher—what actually matters is that they have the skills, determination, and patience needed to help others evolve their game.

To find a coach, I looked on PickleballTeachers .com,[1] which allows prospective students to plug in their locations and get a list of available pickleball coaches in their area, along with their ratings and distances from that specific zip code. (PickleballCentral.com,[2] too, has a solid list of coaches spread out across the country, along with contact info and detailed information about each person's skill set and history.)

I quickly came across Joe Borrelli, an affable, trim man who had a thirty-plus-year career at IBM before retiring in 2012 and who also worked as a youth basketball, baseball, and racquetball coach in both New York and North Carolina. A quick scan at his qualifications—an International Pickleball Teaching Professional Association (IPTPA) Level II certification, six years of coaching under his belt, a 5/5 rating from dozens of reviews—made me certain that he was the right fit for me. (Also, the courts Borrelli taught at were an eight-minute drive from my house in Raleigh, which didn't hurt.)

So, I reached out to him to see if he was available for a session. Before meeting up, he told me some more about his background and strategy, which follows the IPTPA's IDEAS principle of teaching: introduction, demonstration, explanation, activity, and summary. In both his private lessons and group lessons, he said, he works with a mix of beginner- and intermediate-level players, focusing on up to twenty-three specific pickleball skills.

Well, we didn't quite have the time for that (Borrelli was leaving for vacation soon and had a coaching schedule packed to the gills), but he did kindly agree to give me an abbreviated, thirty-minute version of his normal hourlong lessons. A few days later, I laced up my sneakers, put my hair in a ponytail, and headed out to the park.

When I pulled up in the lot, I was surprised to discover six pristine pickleball courts, several of which were already in use by players taking their own lessons or just having some fun. Pickleball, it seemed, was far more popular in my own neighborhood than I'd realized. And Borrelli was clearly thrilled to be there, greeting me with a bag full of paddles and balls slung over his shoulder.

As we walked over to the courts, he asked me about my pickleball experience, or lack thereof. Worried that I was going to embarrass myself during the lesson, I tried to make my limited abilities sound more impressive than they were—only to accidentally call pickleball paddles "racquets" out of nerves and embarrass myself *before* I'd even started playing. (He accepted my harried defense that I really did know the terminology, but I could tell he didn't exactly have the highest expectations about my skills, nor could I blame him.)

Once I had a paddle—not racquet—safely in my hand, Borrelli instructed me to start volleying with him back and forth, standing right at the edge of the Kitchen, so he could get a sense of my basic grasp of the game. Although I needed some corrections—I was using my wrist too much, and my backhand was a mess—we were able to keep things going fairly well, reaching more than fifty dinks before I hit one into the net. Borrelli seemed both relieved and impressed; some beginners he works with, he told me, take more than a week to get to that volley length, while I'd done it in only a few minutes. (Whether he was just saying that to boost my self-esteem was unclear, but I was happy to accept the compliment nonetheless.)

Normally during a lesson, he explained, he'd devote much of the hour to mastering one skill, like dinking, until the student had it down cold, but since our time was limited, he thought it best that we move on to other concepts. For the next fifteen minutes or so, he fed me balls as I stood increasingly farther back on the court, with each round getting a little bit trickier: lower hits, faster moves, greater need for backhand. It was easy to see why Borrelli was so in-demand as a coach. Whenever I made a mistake, he'd pause so he could explain what I'd done, tell me why it didn't work, and demonstrate what I should've done instead (even switching playing hands to accommodate my lefty self). After watching me stretch cross-court to return a far-left hit, for instance, he showed me how to watch the ball and position myself accordingly before it arrived, therefore avoiding last-second swerves and increasing my chances of accurate returns. It all made sense, and as the lesson continued on, I was feeling pretty good about myself—that is, until it was time to practice serving.

Was I the worst pickleball server Borrelli had ever seen? Probably (hopefully) not. But I certainly wasn't good. Despite his best coaching efforts, it took me a *long* time to serve with the proper amount of power and height to get the ball into his service area. When I finally did, though, he was as excited about it as I was, making sure I did it correctly another few times before we wrapped up our lesson. By the time we were done, I was sweaty, tired, and surprisingly proud of myself for how much I'd improved in such a short period of time.

It was all thanks to Borrelli's patient, helpful instruction. "Becoming a coach is more than being a good player, it's being a good teacher," he'd told me during that first, pre-lesson conversation. "A good teacher will have a sound knowledge of the game, be able to communicate with the student, understand how different students learn skills, and must be a lifelong learner himself."

Which, as an avid player, Borrelli most definitely is. His love for the game was evident during our time together, as was his enthusiasm for helping others get better. His efforts have paid off; just recently, he told me, two of his former students competed in their first higher-level (4.0) tournament and took home a silver medal, due in no small part to his coaching.

Participating in pickleball tournaments might not be in my own future—I may have learned to serve, but I'm still a klutz whose favorite form of exercise is playing with her dog—but I do feel far more confident in my skills than I used to, thanks to the lesson. Because as my time with Borrelli made clear, as enjoyable as playing on your own can be, it's hard to really grow your skills in pickleball without the help of a professional.

If you want a one-on-one coach of your own, you can search online like I did, but in some towns and cities where pickleball is particularly popular (try saying that five times fast . . .), it's not an uncommon sight for a communal bulletin board (physical or virtual) to be filled with info sheets from coaches noting their offerings and availability. This can be a great, easy way to connect with a local coach, and you'll probably even be able to get some feedback from other neighborhood players who've worked with them before.

If you don't see any coach listings posted, consider putting up a notice of your own saying that you're looking for a locally based coach. If you're up for it, you can also ask some other players if they know anyone who would be willing to help you out, or even walk up to a talented player you see at the courts and ask *them* if they'd be willing to take you on as a student. Good chance, they'll either say yes or connect you with someone else who can be of service. Pickleball is about teamwork and cooperation, after all; the more you can do to help your fellow players succeed in the sport, the better it is for everyone.

Once you find someone who seems like a fit for your needs, reach out to let them know what it is, exactly, that you hope to work with them on improving. Even if you're a total newcomer to the game just looking to learn the basics, your prospective coach should know any relevant information that might affect the way they teach you, such as if you have a background in racquet sports or have suffered an injury to your shoulder or arm. If there *is* an exact skill or two you want to work on, tell them that—they'll likely devise drills and practices that focus on those specific areas.

If one-on-one coaching isn't your style or isn't available to you, there are plenty of other ways to practice your pickleball and work on your game. Below are some common training options applicable to players at every level.

GROUP TRAINING PROGRAMS

For people who learn best in a group setting (or who just want to enjoy the company of other players), there are dozens of training programs across the country that provide lessons en masse.

Catherine Parenteau, the number-one-ranked pickleball player in women's singles and number-three-ranked player in women's doubles, recently launched a namesake academy alongside her partner and coach, Athena Trouillot. I reached out to the duo to find out more about their new academy and the increased interest in pickleball they're seeing across the country. Over a joint phone call, the women described their experience traveling to cities around the United States offering camps and clinics to players of all ages and talents. While originally, their reasons for creating the academy were primarily financial—"the tournaments and the traveling are not cheap, and so teaching was a way that we could generate extra revenue to help compensate for the extra expenses," explained Trouillot—both of them soon realized there was a genuine need for schools like theirs.

"We found out that there are so many people who play pickleball who, one, have no idea pro pickleball even exists, and two, have no instruction in their area at all—all they have is Google and YouTube in order to try to progress and get better at something they love," Trouillot said. "We wanted to take it to the next level and try to teach all over the country, because our idea is that everyone should have access to great instruction."

Their efforts paid off; today, Trouillot said, "demand is insane" for the academy. "We have people contacting us weekly saying, 'Can you come to my area and do a camp or clinic?'" she said. To manage the requests, she and Parenteau have hired additional instructors and come up with a standardized training program to ensure that students receive the same quality of lessons no matter where they live or who is teaching.

Demand for group training is just as high in other countries, where pickleball continues to rise in popularity. In Canada, for example, one top-rated player and in-demand coach, Steve Deakin, offers a number of clinics and boot camps (in addition to one-on-one lessons). When I reached out to Deakin, the Vancouver-based athlete told me that he initially worked with players of all skill levels, but recently, as interest in his lessons has grown, he's switched his focus to training intermediate and advanced players and hiring other instructors to guide the beginners. "I like to work with that 3.0–4.0 skill level, but I also have to be realistic about where my time is most valuable," he explained, referring to pickleball's rating system (more on that in a later chapter!). "My sweet spot is teaching and training 4.5+ players that are kind of looking to take that next step."

Then there's LevelUp Pickleball,[3] a program offering one-, two-, or three-day camps to players of various skill levels. LevelUp also spans the country, with 100+ camps available in 33 states. Led by pro players Lisa and Wayne Dollard (the latter of whom is also the publisher of *Pickleball Magazine*), LevelUp features drills, competitions, and strategy training during each course. There's also Engage Pickleball,[4] a paddle manufacturing company that also offers the largest pickleball training program in the world, with clinics located across the country. At one of Engage's three-day camps, students receive sixteen hours of training—led by pro Robert Elliott, the global director of training for the IFP—plus a free paddle.

The programs mentioned above are just a few of the many group training options available to players, of course. Do some research to find the one that's best for your location, price range, skill set, and more.

ONLINE PICKLEBALL PROGRAMS

If you're not wed to learning pickleball in-person, you can have an even greater range of choices, as many coaches and schools now provide virtual tutorials for players at all skill levels.

CoachME Pickleball,[5] for instance, lets pickleball fans pay a subscription fee to access monthly videos from pro player and teacher Morgan Evans, in which he tackles an assortment of techniques and strategies. If there's a tip you want to learn that's not currently offered, you can suggest that it be covered in future videos.

When I chatted with Evans over the phone, he told me that the idea for the program, which he runs alongside producer Steve Taylor, came from a desire to "teach the masses without having everyone descend on court."

"It's a good way for me to kind of share the massive amounts of randomness that floats around my head with regards to technique, strategy, and everything else in this game," explained Evans, who has also lent his coaching skills to fellow pros like Tyson McGuffin and Riley Newman as pickleball's first-ever Professional Tour Pickleball Coach.

The first time he and Taylor got together to make videos, they had so many tips to share that they ended up filming twenty episodes' worth of content, sixteen of which they released immediately (these days, subscribers receive two videos each month, along with a few other tutorials and articles free to anyone). With so many lessons available online, CoachME subscribers can spend as much time as they want honing a skill before moving on to the next one on their list.

Similarly, Steve Kennedy,[6] a former professional tennis player turned pickleball player and coach, collaborated with the pickleball website The Pickler to offer a video package that contains more than 140 lessons, equaling more than seven hours of footage, on different aspects of the sport, including advanced strategies and drills. Then there's Prem Carnot,[7] a player, coach, and bestselling author known as "The Pickleball Guru," who offers an online course focusing solely on the pickleball drop shot, one of the trickiest yet most important aspects of the game to master.

If you're not looking for a formal online training program, though, don't discount the value of simply looking up the skills you want to improve and watching readily available tutorials. Steve Deakin, the Canadian player and coach, told me that he relied largely on the Internet for help when he first got involved in the sport. "I went onto YouTube and I googled all sorts of things like doubles strategy and singles strategy, and I analyzed all the pro players at that time like Wes Gabrielsen, Brian Ashworth, and Kyle Yates," he recalled. "That's how I started learning the game, from watching them play."

Scrutinizing these players' moves gave Deakin a "really good head's start" when he went back onto the court, he added—so much so that he was able to compete in his first tournament at the pro level less than a year after first picking up a paddle.

However you decide to go about it—subscribing to an online program, taking a group or one-on-one lesson, or just doing some research—there is no shortage of ways to gain new skills, up your game, and have a whole lot of fun doing it.

STRATEGY

ne of the most common sentiments I heard repeated from the pickleball players and coaches I spoke with was some variation of "pickleball is easy to learn, but it's a whole different story to actually get good." It's true—learning the basics of the game may not take much time, but becoming an adept player who handily wins matches and outwits opponents? That requires a serious amount of effort, both on the court and off.

That said, becoming better at pickleball doesn't have to mean shelling out buckets of money for private lessons or traveling across the country to attend elite clinics. There are lots of at-home

The thing that's unique and makes pickleball so special is that there are two elements to the game. There is the power game, for sure, but there's also the strategic side. And you really need to master both in order to be successful.

—*Justin Maloof, COO at USA Pickleball*

exercises you can do alone (or with a partner) at no cost that can also help you on your path of becoming a stronger player.

SIX GREAT PICKLEBALL DRILLS TO TRY OUT

Drills, a.k.a. exercises focused on specific skills, are crucial for players looking to move up in the ranks, as they force you to repeat a technique over and over until you have it down pat. That means not just doing the exercise for a few hours and moving on, but practicing it for days, or even weeks, at a time, until it's ingrained fully in your muscle memory.

"As a rule of thumb, I try to get players at every level to be flipping the ratio of drilling to playing," said Morgan Evans, the CoachME founder. "It's very tempting to try to get all your practice by just playing the game, but unfortunately, it's a horribly inefficient way to get better at pickleball, especially for players that are taking it seriously."

You can do drills by yourself, with a partner, or even just with a wall, depending on the technique you're trying to perfect; there are countless options you can try. Below are a few of the most popular drills used by pickleball players at all skill levels.

Reflex Training.[1] Stand at the Kitchen line, across from your partner. Have them dink back and forth until, without notice, they send a hard drive directly at you. Try to block the shot without letting it pop up in the air—it will train both your reflexes and your shot technique.

Triangle Dinking.[2] Pick three points on the court that, together, form a triangle. Try to hit each point exactly in sequence, and when you've gotten that, pick a different pattern and try that one instead. This drill will help your aim and your ball control.

Target Hitting.[3] This is an easy drill you can do without a partner. On a wall, use chalk or tape to note the height of a pickleball net (36 inches at the posts, 34 inches at the center). Then create a box (a.k.a. your target) right above that line. Stand back at least seven feet to simulate the non-volley zone and try to hit the ball in the target as consistently as possible. For a slightly more advanced version of this drill, try keeping the ball in the air after each hit, or switch back and forth between your forehand and backhand.

Volley Battle.[4] With a partner, hit the ball back and forth across the net, but don't let it hit the ground. See how long the two of you can keep it up for, focusing on your foot speed and hand-eye coordination.

Third Shot Drop Returns. The third shot drop is one of the most crucial shots to learn in pickleball, so drilling can make a major impact on your ability to deliver it during a game. Stand at the baseline of the court, while your partner is at the Kitchen line. Have them dink balls to you and try to return them using that third shot drop, over and over again until you can do it in your sleep.

Skinny Pickle. If your priority is upping your speed and reflexes, another drill option is to play a full game on one side of the court, also known as "skinny pickle."[5] It will be challenging and force you to move ultra-quickly, but that's the whole point.

After you've mastered one drill, move on to the next until you're a pickleball pro ready to take on any player who comes your way. "For the first five years that I played pickleball, I'd warm up for like, five minutes and then go play," said Zane Navratil, the highly rated men's singles player. "But when I started actually figuring out what I needed to work on, isolating that, and drilling instead of just playing . . . that's what really helped my game."

Even if becoming a professional like Navratil isn't in your plans anytime soon (or ever), there's no reason not to hone your skills as much as possible. After all, as fun as the game may be, the competition can still be fierce—and there's no shame in wanting to beat your opponent during a match! That is why I reached out to several of pickleball's most elite athletes to provide some of the tips and tricks that have helped them become stronger players over the years. Whether it's about the height to hold your paddle, the angle to hit your shots, or where to position yourself on the court, the following pieces of advice are meant to help players at *all* levels—beginner, intermediate, and advanced—majorly up their skills.

FOUR CRUCIAL PREGAME TIPS

Before any game, casual or competitive, make sure to keep these four fundamentals in mind to ensure you start things off in the right mindset and ready to go.

1. **Always Warm Up.** Because it's so fun to play, it's easy to forget that pickleball is an athletic sport like any other, requiring players to run around the court, dive for returns, and deliver shots with precise power and precision, often for hours at a time (if you're playing matches) and with few breaks between points. At that

rate, you're pretty much guaranteed to work up a sweat! To avoid losing steam on the court or, worse, getting injured, make sure to stretch and warm up before starting play. During breaks between games, too, take a few minutes to make sure everything's feeling loose and limber. Many pros recommend doing exercises like arm circles (stretching your arms out on each side, then rotating them both clockwise and counterclockwise several times) and hip rotations (raising your knee while in a standing position, then moving your foot to the side and then back, for each leg). Running (or jogging) is another good way to get in some pre-pickleball cardio, as is marching in place or doing high knees across the court.

2. **Don't Forget to Communicate.** Playing doubles? Then prepare to talk to your partner constantly throughout the game. For each shot that comes over the net, shout out if it's yours or theirs, and let them know if you're running over to their side of the court for any reason. Warn them, too, if a ball they're readying to hit looks like it'll land out of court, so they don't accidentally go for a dead ball.[6]

3. **Treat Pickleball as Its Own Sport.** Because so many pickleball players come from tennis

or other athletic backgrounds, they often treat the two games alike, thinking that the same tactics that helped them win in one sport will work just as well in the other. But in reality, that's not the case at all—and in fact, refusing to view pickleball as its own game can be a big mistake. "There are a lot of players I see who come from tennis, and so they step on the pickleball court and they just start playing tennis out there, but they never actually learn some of the pickleball skills that are really important to being a good player" like dinking and drop shots, said Jessie Irvine, the elite pickleball player and a former tennis champion. Often, she continued, tennis players who move to pickleball put too much power into their hits and too little effort into "the soft game," leading to dead balls and missed returns. It's the same concept as in golf, Irvine said: "It doesn't matter how hard you can hit it. If it takes you ten putts to get into the hole, you're done."

4. **Have Fun.** I know, I know, it's a cliché—but remembering that even the toughest pickleball games are, well, games can do wonders for your playing abilities. "If you take it too serious, then you get uptight, you make stupid mistakes, you do things you normally wouldn't

do," noted Chuck Swann, a Florida-based player who regularly competes in tournaments. Wanting to win is totally fine, but don't let that singular focus trip you up in the heat of the moment.

BASIC STRATEGIES FOR PLAYERS JUST STARTING OUT

In the summer of 2019, Jessie Irvine had only been playing pickleball for around eight months when Ben Johns, the top player on the men's side, asked her to team up with him for the Tournament of Champions (TOC) in Brigham City, Utah. Johns's normal partner for mixed doubles was unable to make it, so he needed a last-minute replacement—and he'd heard that Irvine was a skilled player who'd proven she could hold her own during previous competitions (the fact that she didn't have any partner commitments herself yet, due to her newness to the game, definitely helped).

As honored and excited as Irvine was by the offer, she was also, as she recalled to me over a long phone call, "really nervous." After all, Johns was—and is—one of the best pickleball players in the world, and she feared potentially letting him down on the court. But before their first match, the pro gave her one key piece of advice.

"He was like, 'Jessie, Jessie, it's really easy,'" Irvine recalled, imitating Johns's trademark self-assurance. "'All you have to do is rate balls—if it's below the net, hit it soft. If it's above the net and shoulder height, then hit it hard, and hit it *really* hard.'"

The seemingly simple tip ended up having such an impact that the duo won not only that match, but all the others they played during the tournament. At the end, Irvine and Johns walked away with gold medals— her first from one of the sport's majors.

As their victory shows, pickleball strategies don't have to be complicated to pay off. Below are seven other easy techniques that can make a big difference in your chances of winning a game.

1. **Always Be Ready.** One of the most important rules for all pickleball players is to keep yourself in a ready position with your knees bent, feet shoulder-width apart, and paddle positioned upward so you can return a hit as soon as it arrives. If you've played other sports before, this concept should hopefully feel natural. Irina Tereschenko, one of the top-ranked women's pickleball players in the world, said that when she played a celebrity pickleball game against Olympic swimmer Michael Phelps and football star Larry

Fitzgerald, she was impressed by how well the NFL alum, in particular, remembered to stay in position. "He would keep his hands down and when the ball would come up, in a second he would just punch it," recalled Tereschenko, adding that Fitzgerald was also nimble on his feet and skilled at following the ball. (Phelps, on the other hand, "is motivated now to maybe get a little more experience," she said with a laugh.)

2. **Don't Rush In.** Because pickleball can sometimes be a slow-paced game, it's normal for players looking to score a quick point to rush into a serve or return, often resulting in easy, avoidable mistakes. So, before even arriving on the court, remind yourself to be patient. "You'll still get anxious about speeding the ball up or trying to score a point fast, but it's about waiting for the opportunity to score," said Tyson Apostol, a four-time *Survivor* contestant and cohost of *PicklePod*, a pickleball-themed podcast. The same sentiment, he continued, applies if your opponents have sped up the ball themselves, and it's your turn to respond. "Rather than take wild swings at it or try to keep the ball moving fast, slow it down and reset and try it

again when the opportunity presents itself," said Apostol.

3. **Focus on Accuracy, Not Power.**[7] As tempting as it is to hit the ball with all of your might every time, that's not necessarily going to increase the speed of your shots, and in fact it can give your opponents an easier chance to score on their return. "If all [a player] can do is hit it hard, you're just gonna be there ready to block it and slow it down," explained Apostol. Instead, work on sending accurate, consistent shots, especially when you're serving— because remember, if you botch a serve in pickleball, you don't get another chance.

4. **Send Your Shots Deep.** An easy way to mess with your opponent is to return shots toward the baseline, forcing them to run back and, soon after, rush back to the net. You can also try aiming shots at the middle of the court, an area where both of your opponents (when playing doubles) might not know who's covering.

5. **Go for Arcs, Not Lobs.** Lobs are undoubtedly fun shots, but they don't always work, and perfecting the lob technique takes a lot of time and practice. Consider focusing your efforts instead on arcs, softer shots that go

high on your side of the court and then land right into your opponent's Kitchen.

6. **Don't Wait for a Bounce.** A key tip that Joe Borrelli taught me during our one-on-one lesson is that while, yes, you *can* let the ball bounce before returning a hit, it's often smarter to avoid it when possible. The reason? When you back up to get behind the ball after a bounce, you're forced to change position, therefore wasting valuable time you could be spending thinking about how and where you're going to return the shot. Speaking of positioning—many players recommend standing as close to the Kitchen line as possible throughout a game unless you're serving, in which case you should stand back at the baseline.

7. **Become an Expert at Dinking.** Dinking, a.k.a. hitting the ball slowly and softly from the Kitchen line, may not be the most exciting or fanciest pickleball technique, but it *is* the most important. "Slowing the game down is essential," explained Apostol, because the longer the game, the more chances there are for your opponents to mess up. So, before trying to learn drop shots and drives, make sure you have dinking down pat. When lining

up for a shot, keep your knees bent, stabilize your elbow and wrist, and swing from your shoulder. This will ensure a solid dink that will keep the game alive and your opponents on the alert.

FIVE MIDLEVEL STRATEGIES FOR PLAYERS READY TO GET COMPETITIVE

Once you've mastered the basics, it's time to work on fine-tuning your skills and perfecting shots that will leave your opponents in the wind.

1. **Aim for Your Opponent's Backhand (and Perfect Your Own).** For most players, their backhand is a lot weaker than their forehand, so take advantage of this by sending shots that your opponent will be forced to return via backhand.[8] If they're right-handed, for instance, then aim for their left foot, which would require them to use backhand to return. This isn't to say, however, that you shouldn't also be working on strengthening your own backhand, as you don't want your opponents to catch on to your trick and send shots you struggle to return.

2. **Finesse Your Drop Shots.** Drop shots[9] (also known as third shot drops, because they come

after a serve and return-serve) are tricky to perfect, but that's what makes them so deadly. They're best used when your opponents are at the non-volley line and you're near the baseline, because if you're the serving team, this positioning will give you a perfect opportunity to send the other team a soft, gentle shot that will land right in their Kitchen. And while they attempt to return the shot upward so it clears the net, you and your partner can run to your own Kitchen and get ready to respond to what's likely a soft, easy-to-return dink.

3. **Don't Overmove Your Wrist.** During my own pickleball lesson, I leaned heavily on my wrist to do all the action until Joe Borelli pointed out how ineffective that strategy was and corrected my form. As it turns out, many players—even higher-level athletes—have made the same mistake. When I spoke to Preston Bies, a spikeball champion and all-around athlete (including in pro-level pickleball), he told me that even he assumed that he'd get more topspin if he snapped his wrist right as he hit the ball, sort of like in tennis. Yet as he was quickly informed by some of the world's top pickleball players, that's not actually the case. "Something

that is always reminded to me by the all-pros is, let the paddle face do all the spin work and angle," Bies said. "During the shot and post-shot, you shouldn't flick the wrist too much. Really, your wrist shouldn't be doing anything besides being manipulated prior to the shot."

4. **Learn from Other Players.** As you develop your own skills on the court, don't forget to keep an eye on what your opponents and teammates are doing, as well. If you see a shot or technique you're particularly impressed by, take some time afterward to think about how it was set up, what effort it required, and why it was used (you can always ask the person who did it for their tips and insight, as well, of course). Once you've gotten a good understanding of how the skill works, practice it frequently as a drill to refine your technique before eventually trying it out in a game or tournament. On that note . . .

5. **Sign Up for Tournaments.** If you've never done it before, the idea of playing pickleball in an actual tournament can sound pretty terrifying. But if you're hoping to become a serious player, there's no better way to do it than by throwing yourself right into a competition, since you'll be surrounded by

other competitive athletes. Don't worry too much about winning at first; focus instead on getting as much experience, and exposure to other players, as possible.

THREE STRATEGIES FOR PLAYERS LOOKING TO GO FROM GOOD TO GREAT

You play pickleball nearly every day, regularly win games against friends, and are now itching to show the world that you're the best player you can be. Here's how to get there.

1. **Strengthen Your Defense.** Sending hard-to-return shots and perfecting your serve can get you far, but offensive strategy shouldn't be your only priority. "Where you separate a lot of these 4.5–5.0s to the pros," said Steve Deakin, the Canadian champ, "is what sort of defense you can come up with when you're caught midcourt." That may mean moving up to the Kitchen line so you have extra time to return a shot, or racing to another side of the court to prepare for where you think your opponents' hit might land. The more you play, the more you'll learn, and the better defensive player you'll become.

2. **Work on Deception.** Similarly, a top pickleball player should always be brainstorming ways to misdirect their opponents and cause them to mess up, said Deakin. Before returning a shot, think carefully about where they might not be expecting it to land, or aim it at the player you think will be weakest upon return. Additionally, if you're known for using a particular technique or serve, consider switching things up before your next game. "People get used to your strategy and playing style," explained Tereschenko. "Try to think, 'What do I need to do to create more deception?'"

3. **Play the Percentages.** The phrase "playing the percentages" means using data and experience to make a decision that has the strongest chance of success, and it can be applied to competitive pickleball. If you have a killer drop shot, say, use it as much as possible during a game to up your chances of winning points, rather than trying out other types of shots that may be exciting but not as reliable for you. Similarly, if you know you can return a shot with an easy dink rather than a more powerful hit, go for the former—the more complicated the shot, the more likely you'll accidentally make a mistake.[10]

In addition to all these strategies, you probably have some of your own that have served you well during games so far. Practice them, share them, and—if you're ready—show them off on the tournament court.

My mixed-doubles partner and I were playing in a tournament, and we were down 10–1. The other team had 10 points, and so they were at game point. And you always say, "Hey, we still got a chance, we still got a shot," but you don't believe it half the time. But we slowly came back, and we wound up winning the game 12–10. That was a big deal—and we ultimately won the match.

—Chuck Swann, 3.0-level player and technical sales manager

6

COMPETITIONS

Like many eight-year-olds with too much energy and very patient parents, Jack Loughridge has spent much of his childhood switching between sports: tennis lessons one afternoon, soccer practice on another. He enjoyed playing both, and was good enough at them to rack up a significant amount of trophies and medals. But it wasn't until he discovered pickleball while at summer camp in 2021 that the Las Vegas–based third grader realized his true athletic passion lay elsewhere.

I met Jack through USA Pickleball, which had recently highlighted him and some other young players making a splash in the Juniors pickleball world. With help from his mom, Courtney, we scheduled a Zoom call for an afternoon after school, and over the course of thirty (fidgety) minutes, I learned firsthand just how much Jack loves the sport—and how impressively quickly he's risen in its ranks.

For starters: Back at home after camp following that first summer, he began working with a pickleball coach to learn shots and strategy, while continuing to play his other sports simultaneously. "We did a lesson of tennis one week and then a lesson of pickleball one week," recalled Courtney, sitting next to her son during the video chat. "And then pretty soon he said, 'I don't want to do any more tennis, just all pickleball.'"

After that, Jack started spending hours each day at a local court and taking now-weekly lessons. Occasionally he attends a clinic with pickleball-playing friends like a classmate, Dean, who Jack discovered during school one day loved pickleball as much as he did. ("It turns out they're both little pickleball addicts," said Courtney.) Sometimes Jack is joined by his dad, Bret, who took up the game when he realized his son needed a partner; Courtney plays, too, but Jack, highly skeptical of her claim to be "pretty good," told both of us that he'll only consider partnering with her if she and Bret do it first, "to see how you are."

With so much time and effort devoted to pickleball, it wasn't long before Jack became skilled enough to qualify for his first official tournament. At the Junior PPA Championships in Las Vegas that October—just two months after he'd started playing—he competed against other young players and took home a bronze medal. By the end of the year, he had several more tournaments under his belt, another medal (silver, this time), and a growing ambition to get better and better at the game he loved.

Most of the time, Jack's wins have been against other children, albeit ones several years his senior—"you're always the youngest kid out there," Courtney proudly noted to him on our call—but increasingly often, he finds himself defeating adults, too. USA Pickleball rules[1] stipulate that juniors can play in adult brackets if the other player is over eighteen, so at times, Jack and his dad partner up for doubles. Nearly always, he's the only child on the court; even when there are other father-son teams playing in a league, the next-youngest members are in their mid-twenties.

If the elementary schooler is ever intimidated by going up against players many times his age, he doesn't show it. "If they're a higher level, it could be a big game, but if they're lower level, it could be an easy game," Jack said matter-of-factly. Besides, he added, the age disparity sometimes gives him the upper hand on the court. At one recent local tournament, for instance, his adult opponents, likely assuming he couldn't handle a real adult game, focused their energies solely on his dad. "If they had a chance to smack the ball, they would smack it at my dad and not me," he recalled, a big smile on his face. "That was really fun."

Overall, though, he prefers playing against the younger set, both because of the lower difficulty level and the opportunity to meet fellow pickleball-loving kids. One pal, a "really good" player named Leo from Park City, Utah, has become a frequent companion at adult tournaments, while another, Dublin, is the only friend Jack has lost to so far ("but it was a good match," he said diplomatically).

That single loss aside, Jack's talent has grown to a point that going up against the under-ten-set is not always the most satisfying experience for him. At a Juniors tournament in Utah, for instance, he was paired with a weaker partner, forcing him to perform double duty on the court. "It was mostly me that was doing the work," he said with evident frustration, before making sure to add, "in singles I did good, because it's only me."

Whoever he goes up against next and whatever age they are, it's clear that they'll be facing off against a serious contender—especially now that Jack has a pickleball court in his backyard to practice on, a decision his parents made once they realized how seriously he was taking the sport. Well, not *that* seriously. "Pickleballs are falling out of the car constantly because he plays with them in the car, and there's always a paddle out," Courtney said, laughing. "Mom always says, 'Put your paddle back in your bag!'"

"It's fun, though, because he really does love it," she continued. "We're always like, 'Do it if you want to do it or don't,' and he always wants to do it."

And, as Jack told me, he wants to keep doing it as long as he can. "My goal is probably to get a gold medal with my dad in doubles," he said, a statement that surprised his mom. He added that he also wants to perfect his "tweener" shot, a.k.a. an advanced-level shot hit between a player's legs with their back to the net. "I can do it at the Kitchen line, but not over my head," he explained.

Just don't expect Courtney to help him out on the court. "You gotta give me a chance," she implored one last time during our call, but Jack just shrugged and smiled, clearly content to stay the top pickleball player in the family.

While Jack's road to stardom may be an unusual one, his desire to compete in tournaments and show off his abilities is par for the course for thousands of pickleball players worldwide. Each year, people of all skill and experience levels participate in the hundreds of official competitions put on by pickleball organizations. Some of the most well-known include the twenty competitions that are part of the Professional Pickleball Association (PPA) Tour, a lineup of more than two dozen professional pickleball tournaments spread out throughout the year in United States and Canada. These events lead up to pickleball's five majors, some of the most prestigious and highly attended tournaments in the sport (along with non-PPA events like the U.S. Open Pickleball Championships, which is the largest pickleball tournament in the world, and the Margaritaville USA Pickleball National Championships, held at California's renowned Indian Wells Tennis Garden). There's also the Association of Pickleball Professionals (APP) Tour, which has its own esteemed lineup of yearly tournaments that culminates with their season-ending APP Masters.

For many players, much of the appeal of these tournaments is the opportunity to win big—medals, yes, but for the most elite of the bunch, money, too. The 2021 Margaritaville Championships, for instance, offered a total of $90,000 in prize money[2] to medalists (a steep increase from previous years, thanks largely to sponsors), and through both its tournaments and masters, the PPA Tour will award more than $3 million to its pro divisions in 2022, according to Hannah Johns, the organization's head of content.

Unlike in most other sports, the prize money at PPA-sanctioned tournaments is equal for both male and female athletes, a long-held policy that was enacted by the organization to ensure that pickleball continues to be an inclusive space for all players. This commitment to equality extends to the PPA's appearance fees for the game's top pros, which are the same across sexes, as well.

In addition to the potential of prizes and bragging rights, tournaments also give players the chance to spend a few days (or even a week) bonding with other pickleball fans and sharing in their passion with the rest of the sport's community. Jennifer Lucore, the player and pickleball historian who spoke to me about the sport's early days, told me that half the fun of competing in these events is everything that occurs off the court. "Just the journey to the pickleball tournaments is fun in and of itself—all the shenanigans that happen like the car trips, the photos," she said. "And then afterwards, going to dinner with all the people you just played against and tried to beat up on."

Over the past few years, as tournament participation by both players and spectators has grown, many organizers have made changes to their events' formats and offerings to ensure that attendees get the most out of their time there. The PPA, for instance, recently increased the number of games in a match from three to five, in order to build greater suspense for viewers; and thanks to an influx of funding from sponsors, they've also been able to level up in their nongame entertainment offerings for fans like on-court giveaways, food vendors, merch sales, and music by a DJ.

Terri Graham, from the U.S. Open Pickleball Championships, said that she and her copresident and cofounder Chris Evon have made a concentrated effort over the past few years to turn the competition into a fun-filled destination for fans of the sport. "We wanted to make it a party first, and a tournament second," she explained. Not that they've had to do much work; Graham said that due to the sheer amount of attendees each year—many of whom come in large groups and rent out Airbnb's for the week—the championships automatically becomes "a huge celebration."

On a typical day, she continued, attendees will compete in or watch a match before heading off the courts to explore downtown Naples, meet up with other players, and party well into the night—all before repeating it again the next day, and the day after that. "You hear a lot, 'This was on my bucket list to come here,'" Graham said.

Indeed, many pickleball fans will happily travel across their state, country, or even the world to attend tournaments, whether as competitors, spectators, or, often, both.

Laura Gainor, the USA Pickleball marketing consultant, has spent most of her weekends over the past few years traveling to tournaments across the country for "pickleball getaways" alongside a group of female friends, she told me. On each trip, the women split their time between competing in events and exploring the local area, making memories as they share in their love of the sport. "We get a hotel and have such a great time," she said.

Some tournament attendees spend their time at the competitions taking on roles as volunteers, helping organizers with everything from tracking down players to coordinating shuttles. At the U.S. Open, Graham told me, nearly three hundred volunteers—some of whom have helped out at the competition every year since it began in 2016—are needed to help the weeklong event run smoothly. "They are our pride and joy," she said of the group. "They make the U.S. Open what it is."

Other players, meanwhile, contribute by taking on roles as referees, overseeing tournaments' medal and pro-level matches. Not anyone can just hop in the chair; prospective referees undergo extensive training and several tests before earning their official titles. But those who do make the cut play a huge part in helping to keep pickleball competitions organized and enjoyable for all participants.

Then there are the efforts put in by the attendees themselves—including even tournaments' highest-rated players, many of whom take time out of their schedules to hang out with fans in between matches, signing autographs and chatting about strategy. Because tournaments are usually several days long while the actual pickleball competition periods are fairly condensed, players have plenty of time to socialize with their peers, idols, or fans.

Steve Deakin, the Canadian pro, recalled to me how at the 2019 National Championships, he and fellow player Erik Lange found themselves competing in the gold medal match against two of the sport's very best players, Ben Johns and Kyle Yates. Despite an impressive showing, the underdogs ended up falling short of victory. But what Deakin remembers most from that tournament is not the loss, but the support he received from a stadium packed full of fans and fellow players cheering him on.

"I've played in front of some large crowds before," he told me. "But the energy and atmosphere in that stadium . . . it took my breath away. It literally gave me goose bumps when I walked onto the court."

That special connection between players and fans is undoubtedly due in part to pickleball's uniquely intimate setup. Because of the high number of annual tournaments, players get to see each other quite often, with the most serious individuals finding themselves competing together dozens of times throughout the year. Zane Navratil, the men's singles pro, said during our Zoom call that he feels that the frequency of events leads to stronger connections between players. "There's a sense of camaraderie because you see the same people—and it's a small group of people—week in and week out," he explained. In tennis, he added, the limited number of tournaments and bigger pool of players means that "you might play somebody five times in a given year," and not get to know most of your competitors well, if at all. Not in pickleball, though; Navratil said that he and his fellow top player Jay Devilliers have competed against each other "twenty-seven times" over the last year.

This unique setup brings the pickleball community closer and allows relationships between players to thrive. Yet while pickleball fans at all levels enter tournaments to have a good time and connect with others, that isn't to say that they aren't also there to win, of course. After all, who doesn't want to walk away from a competition with a medal in their hands, or even just the satisfaction of having taken down a tough opponent?

Navratil, for one, still lights up remembering the January 2021 tournament—his first as a professional player—in which he edged out the top two men's players in the game at the time, Ben Johns and Tyson McGuffin. "Nobody else had really broken through and beaten those guys in a couple of years," he told me on our call, smiling. "But I did."

Tournaments aren't only for pickleball's elite, though. The majority of matches at competitions are between amateur players, including some who've only picked up a paddle for the first time a few months (or weeks!) before. Dave Gould, a landlord (and a pal of a family friend), traveled a few years ago from his home of Saratoga Springs, New York, to Colorado Springs, Colorado, in order to play in his first-ever tournament. Over the course of several days, he and his partner faced off against a series of increasingly challenging competitors, conquering each game and, eventually, their competition bracket overall. "Winning it was a rush of euphoria," Gould said. "It made the trip from New York to Colorado all worth it."

In any pickleball tournament, brackets are broken down not just by age and gender (except for mixed doubles, a popular category) but by skill levels, with players in the same rating group facing off against each other to ensure equal games. Speaking of ratings—in competitive pickleball (even just within more casual leagues and clubs), each player's skill is determined by where they fall on a scale of 1.0–5.0. While some clubs and leagues give ratings to their members, most pickleball players self-rate, using the abbreviated criteria below (the full rubric[3] is available on USA Pickleball's site) to determine where they stand.

1.0–2.0—A player at this level is just starting out, with no sports background or understanding of pickleball's rules.

2.5—A player with this ranking has a bit of experience playing the game, a basic understanding of how to keep score, and the ability to have a short, sustained rally with other players at the same level.

3.0—At 3.0, the requirements start getting more specific. A player here understands the main rules and positioning of pickleball, can hit medium-paced shots using their forehand, and is able to serve, return a serve, and volley. They don't have to have mastered using their backhand or be able to keep up a dink rally, though, as they probably don't yet have much control and consistency in their hits. A 3.0 player should also be starting to compete in tournaments.

3.5—This level player has developed a better (if not great) sense of depth control and accuracy with their shots, and can now use their backhand moderately well and sustain moderate-length dink rallies. They also are working on the third drop shot, regularly

COMPETITIONS

117

moving up toward the Kitchen, and starting to understand how much power each individual shot requires.

4.0—A player with a 4.0 rating has a solid understanding of play and positioning, working in tandem with their partner on the court. The accuracy and timing of their shots are mostly consistent, and they're learning when and when not to go after a ball. They're also beginning to get into strategy, formulating game plans against their opponents and seeking out opportunities to attack.

4.5—To be rated 4.5, a player hits largely consistent and intentional shots (including overhead shots), while also varying their techniques based on their opponents' positioning and attacks. They play both offensively and defensively, often executing third shot drops that aren't easily returned and making few errors. They're quick on their feet and communicate well, utilizing stacking (a.k.a. rearranging their team's positioning on the court to keep one player in a certain spot) whenever it's needed.

5.0—5.0 players are highly-skilled, making easy and effective use of their footwork and positioning throughout a game. They've mastered all shot types (with both forehand and backhand) and vary them frequently, based on their opponents' moves at any given moment. They rarely make errors, have a strong grasp on strategy, and are just as capable of going on the attack as they are blocking shots.

5.5+—As said, only an extremely small number of pros have a 5.5 or higher rating. These players are at the absolute top of their game, handily winning tournaments and consistently performing at peak levels. In other words, they're the very best there is.

If you're in doubt at all about where you fall on the scale, consider asking some experienced, already-ranked players to weigh in on your abilities and help you find the correct spot. Keep in mind, too, that if you plan to compete in multiple tournament categories (that is, singles, doubles, or mixed doubles), then you'll need a separate rating for each one, since your abilities can vary depending on the format. If your skill level changes, you can update your rating as needed, but if you're competing in tournaments, it will likely be changed automatically. PickleballTournaments.com,[4] the software used by USA Pickleball to keep tabs on competitions, constantly adjusts players' ratings based on their results, ensuring that they're placed in the right categories for future events. Once you compete in your first tournament, you can make a profile on the site, and the software will take things from there.

You can also use the site (or its app) to view the listings of upcoming tournaments and find one that seems like a good match for your needs. You can search based on location, date, or a keyword (like *senior* or *beach*), and once you find an event that piques your curiosity, check out the details for more insight on what to expect. Most tournament listings include important information like how many days they run for, what the age requirement is for participants (if there is one), what events will be featured, and which players have already signed up to compete. You can usually register on the spot; the entrance fee for each tournament varies, but it's typically fairly minimal, around $40–$60 (and there's often a discount for early birds).

Once you've signed up for a tournament, add your name to the bracket(s) you want to compete in—you can pick as many as you qualify for. Just make sure that you're familiar (or will be, by the time the competition comes around) with the rules and format of each match.[5] Also keep in mind that if you're planning on playing doubles, you'll need a partner, but you don't have to have someone already picked out. There's always a list of players also looking for partners available to peruse, and you can find and contact a potential match from there.[6]

If the tournament will feature any element different from what you're used to, like an indoor court instead of outdoor, spend some time after registration getting acclimated with it so you won't be thrown off during competition. And start packing your bags; bring sunscreen if the event is outdoors, extra shoes and socks to prevent blisters, some spare clothes or a towel for if you get sweaty between matches, and of course, paddles and balls (you'll want to have several of both as backups).

And of course, get practicing! Even if it's your first-ever tournament, fit in plenty of matches and drills, as you don't want to show up to compete with anything other than your A-game. That idea should go for your pre-competition diet, too.

To get an expert opinion on what that consumption should ideally look like, I reached out to Barbara Lewin, a sports nutritionist who frequently works with top pickleball players. "Your best health and nutrition will give you your best performance," she explained. "In no way," though, she was quick to add, "should you restrict calories prior to play—even if you're trying to lose weight." Instead, she said, focus on choosing energy-enhancing meals low in fat and fiber, like toasted bagels with jam or egg whites.

When packing your bags, throw in some snacks, too, because you may not have time before or between matches to grab a healthy meal. Lewin recommends "easy to digest" items like bananas, pretzels, or even fat-free chocolate milk (for after a game, since many brands are specifically aimed at post-exercise recovery). Don't forget drinks; hours spent running around the court means that you'll need plenty of water to keep you fueled. "I've seen paramedics more than once being called for players who became overheated or dehydrated," said Lewin.

Catherine Parenteau, the number-one-rated women's singles player, said that in the days leading up to a tournament, she drinks "a lot of water and electrolytes" to ensure she's as hydrated as possible. On the morning of a competition, she supplements her beverages with a wheat bagel with peanut butter and bananas, and she brings rice cakes, fruits, and bars to snack on during the day. (A typical post-tournament dinner, she added, is full of proteins, carbs, and vegetables.)

Not having to worry about what you're going to eat at the tournament also means that you'll have more time when you arrive to familiarize yourself with the event's setup ahead of your first match. After that, warm up, either on an empty court with your partner or at one of the pre-tournament clinics commonly offered at events. Just don't forget to keep your ears peeled for the referee calling out your match and court number, so you don't accidentally keep your competitors (and the whole tournament) waiting.

As for the matches themselves, don't worry too much if you don't win your first one; all pickleball tournaments guarantee players a minimum of two matches. Depending on the format of that particular tournament (such as single or double elimination, round robin, etc.), an early loss might send you down a bracket and/or take you out of the running for the very top prizes, but you'll always still get the chance to redeem yourself in at least one more round. Jack Loughridge, for example, won his silver medal at the 2021 Duel in the Las Vegas Desert tournament despite losing his first two games, due to the high number of points he accumulated overall.

Even if you don't make it too far in competition, though, stick around until the end of the tournament if you can, because that's usually when medals are distributed and final celebrations occur. But if you're unable to stay, you don't have to miss out on the fun; these days, most major tournaments are streamed live on TV and online. Tell your friends and family back at home to watch, too, because the more people that tune into tournaments, the bigger the events will be able to grow, and the better experiences they'll be for every person involved—pros, newbies, and everybody in between.

We'd travel to the three biggest tournaments, and I would always get fourth or fifth, super close to the podium but never *on* the podium. And at one point, I kind of got sick of it and said, "I need to change. I'm super competitive—I don't want to get fourth or fifth. That's not good enough for me. I really want to perform better." So I just started drilling a lot more than actually playing, and it made a big difference with my results in my performance. . . . I was able to win the U.S. Open in Naples last year in women's doubles.

—Catherine Parenteau, professional player
and cofounder of the Catherine Parenteau
Pickleball Academy

GOING PRO

For many serious pickleball players, the hope of one day turning pro—in other words, playing in the highest-level tournament brackets, catching the attention of sponsors, and bringing in serious money—is the driving force behind their efforts on the court. Yet it wasn't all that long ago that the professional side of the sport didn't even exist.

According to Terri Graham, the U.S. Open cofounder, there were no professional pickleball players as recently as 2016, due to the lack of major tournaments and sponsorships for pickleball's top players. Instead, these athletes were referred to simply by their rating, preventing more casual fans of the sport from understanding their skill and companies from backing them financially. Because of this lack of recognition, most early pros were forced to view pickleball—despite their significant talents and efforts—as little more than a hobby, with no intention of turning it into a career.

Catherine Parenteau, for instance, now the top-rated women's single player, originally took up the sport merely as a fun side activity. "When we first got into pickleball, we were just thinking it was just a fun sport to do on the side, and nothing really serious was going to come out of it," she recalled, speaking for herself and her partner and coach, Athena Trouillot. "We were playing for fun, maybe competing in little tournaments, but never thinking of it as a professional sport."

To supplement their incomes, Parenteau and Trouillot took on "day jobs" in addition to the many hours devoted to pickleball, which the athlete said was as exhausting as it sounds. After long days teaching in Naples country clubs, they would fly out to Arizona or another state to compete in a tournament for a few days, before coming back and resuming their lessons right away.

Jennifer Lucore, the player and pickleball historian, remembered a not-so-distant time when even at the biggest competitions like Nationals, a winner back in the day was lucky if they made "maybe five hundred bucks" from prize money. Sponsorship funds weren't much better; when Lucore was chosen by Pickle-Ball Inc. to be the sport's first ever sponsored player, the financial benefit was minimal, to say the least. The company paid for her travel and tournament entry fees, the latter of which rarely amounted to more than thirty dollars.

Motivated by their love for the game and desire to see it grow, though, early pickleball pros continued forth, despite the money (or lack thereof). And luckily, once the PPA and APP tours formed in 2018, creating organized rosters of tournaments with funding behind them and TV networks interested in streaming the events, the sport's professional side took off for real. Today, thanks to this support, pickleball's most elite players are steadily building large fan bases and earning sizable sponsorships.

It's a very tiny percentage of players doing this, to be certain. Like in any sport, the number of pickleball players who are considered professionals is low, and the number of *them* who do manage to earn enough from prize money and sponsorships to support their careers is even smaller. Even established professional players like Parenteau have their hands full. Despite having earned enough success through pickleball to hire a full team of support staff, she still spends her days running just as chaotically between tournaments, clinics, and training sessions as she did early on. "It's a lot of work," she admitted.

"Slowly," though, she added, "we're trying to learn how to transition into being full-time pickleball."

The game's leading organizations are helping. In January, the APP announced a partnership with sports marketing giant Intersport to increase prize money and appearance fees for pickleball pros.[1] Similarly, the PPA recently started forming exclusivity agreements with many top athletes that not only require them to limit their tournaments to stops on the tour, but guarantee them celebrity-level treatment at all tour events. The contracts ensure that these competitions offer appearance fees for pro players and treat them well, in addition to taking care of their logistical needs like parking and, importantly, the existence of separate places where they can get away and relax after a match. "Because at this point," explained Hannah Johns, the PPA's head of content, "we're getting to a point where the pros get so harassed at the venue by fans for autographs, pictures, wanting to talk to them."

Not that the increased interest from spectators is a bad thing. "The number one thing that we're really trying to strive for now is just trying to help the sport, but also the athletes, become a little more mainstream," added Connor Pardoe, the PPA commissioner. "That's the next big step for us, helping some of these players really be professional athletes *and* professional celebrities."

Indeed, while pickleball's top players may not yet have the household name recognition of, say, Roger Federer or Serena Williams, the backing they have from major brands, plus support from thousands of loyal fans across the world, means they may be well on their way. And as pickleball's popularity continues to rise, with more attention and money going into the sport every day, its pros' platforms will only get bigger, as well.

Yet no matter how much money they make or medals they earn, pickleball's most elite players are driven by one primary thing: their deep, enduring love of the game. Every single pro I spoke to for this book was proud to tell me how much work they do behind the scenes to spread word of the sport, whether by training new players, creating leagues and clinics, or, in the case of one top athlete you'll read about later in this chapter, even traveling to other countries to help jump-start pickleball programs abroad. While their ages, backgrounds, and specialties vary, each of these pros is bonded by their commitment to giving the sport their all both on *and* off the court.

Below, get to know three of pickleball's highest-ranked players, all of whom have dedicated countless hours of their life not just to mastering the game, but to sharing it with the world.

JESSIE IRVINE

Age: 32

Hometown: Cary, North Carolina

Claim to Fame: Fourth-rated player in women's doubles

Jessie Irvine always knew she was going to be a professional athlete. As a kid, the future pickleball champion had a knack for tennis that earned her the ranking of one of the top ten junior players in the country, and she spent much of her adolescence in North Carolina honing her skills and handily winning matches. A career as a pro player seemed not just possible, but assured—until the teen started experiencing frequent, severe joint pain while training at prestigious tennis academies.

Tests found that Irvine had been born with very little cartilage in her joints, and while a lack of broken bones growing up meant that she'd been able to go years without knowing she had the condition, the movements and power required for serving in her level of tennis had led to pinched nerves. Doctors warned Irvine that continuing to play the sport would result in more issues, but the teen, determined to achieve her goal of becoming an adult professional player, refused to stop.

After a few years of trying to move up in the ranks while dealing with the pain, though, Irvine made the difficult choice to step away from the world of competitive tennis, as her body just couldn't handle it anymore. Needing time to process the decision, she took a few years off from tennis completely, only coming back to it at the age of twenty-one after a cross-country move to Los Angeles. There she started teaching tennis to kids, a career path she found herself loving so much she kept at it for more than ten years.

Eventually, encouraged by some tennis-loving friends, Irvine got back into the sport, competing in casual matches every now and then. When those pals introduced to her a game called paddle tennis (also known as pop tennis), involving a punctured tennis ball, a foam paddle, and a beach court, she started playing that, too.

In November 2018, after noticing how much Irvine seemed to be taking to paddle tennis, her friends told her about a *third* sport she might enjoy, pickleball. This one, they said, was not only fun to play and growing increasingly popular, but had far more opportunities for competition and tournaments—two things Irvine was greatly missing—than her other activities.

Intrigued, Irvine gave pickleball a try. Unsurprisingly, she became an immediate fan, and as her talent increased, higher-ranked players started asking her to partner with them—for Irvine, this was the telltale sign that she had what it took to go far in the sport. Just a few months after first picking up a paddle, she decided to pursue pickleball professionally.

"Things just happened really quickly from there," the player recalled to me over the phone. Over the course of 2019, she entered and placed in numerous pickleball tournaments, including a gold medal win at the Margaritaville National Championships. By the end of the year, Irvine had climbed up the game's ranks faster than most athletes do over their entire careers; today, at thirty-three, she's one of the top women's pickleball players in the world, in addition to being a coach who shares her talents at clinics and training camps across the country.

To keep herself at the top of her game, Irvine sticks to doubles and mixed doubles, noting that the effort required in a one-on-one game isn't good for her joints. "[Singles games] are a lot tougher on the body," she explained. "And I'm trying to play pickleball as long as I can."

That means not just adjusting her needs during play, but taking care of herself off-court, too. When Irvine isn't competing in a tournament or teaching the game to pickleball newbies, she's attending physical therapy and doing drills to keep her body healthy. After her heartbreaking experience with tennis, she doesn't take her new career—and the ability to simply participate in a sport she loves—for granted. "It's given me a second chance to be competitive again, which was cut short for me with tennis," the athlete said. "I'm extremely grateful for that, and I see it as a blessing."

The fact that her loved ones have front-row seats to her success—such as a double gold medal win at the 2021 PPA Championships in Las Vegas, Irvine's best-ever tournament result—just adds to that appreciation. "My family sacrificed a lot to help me achieve my tennis dreams," Irvine explained. "But then not being able to follow through with that, you feel like, 'My family went through all these sacrifices and then nothing kind of came from it.'"

Now, though, her family not only can watch her win tournaments, but also can witness how thrilled she is to finally have the professional athletic career she's always wanted.

"They're super supportive. They love it, they get into it, they're cheering me on," said Irvine. "I think it's just given me another spark of fire to the flame of just being able to compete again."

ZANE NAVRATIL

Age: 26
Hometown: Racine, Wisconsin
Claim to Fame: Second-rated player in men's singles

Like Irvine, Zane Navratil comes from a competitive tennis background; as a teenager, he won his division's tennis state championships not once, but three times. So when he first learned about pickleball as an eighteen-year-old, he was confident that he could easily take on any opponent who came his way, and wary that the game was even worth his time. "I thought it was an old person's sport," he recalled when we chatted over our Zoom call. "I had no interest in playing."

Yet the first time Navratil tried out pickleball at the local community center where his dad had "dragged" him to play, the high schooler found himself in severely over his head. Or, as he put it more matter-of-factly eight years later, "I got my butt kicked."

Competing against three significantly older men—it was seniors-only time at the community center—Navratil tried to use his tennis skills to his advantage, only to find that he was no match for his talented opponents. "I was like, 'What on earth is happening to me right now?'" the now-twenty-six-year-old remembered thinking, chuckling at the memory.

Determined not to repeat the embarrassing loss, he committed himself to learning the ins and outs of pickleball, "falling in love with it in the process," as he recalled. In college at the University of Wisconsin–Whitewater, he studied accounting and played tennis while continuing to work on his pickleball skills. After graduation, he got a job as an auditor with Deloitte, working long hours and competing in local tournaments on the side (often with his dad, a solid player himself). Frequently he competed alongside another Wisconsin pickleball player, Dave Weinbach, whose impressive turns at events around the country—including several U.S. Open and Nationals gold medal wins—inspired Navratil to up his own game. "I would play a lot with him, and I could beat him sometimes," he said. "So I figured, 'Hey, if this guy's winning national championships and I'm right there with him, I think I can make it happen as well.'"

Over the next several years, Navratil entered many higher-level tournaments, earning enough success to make his way far up the national rankings. By the time the pandemic hit in early 2020, his pickleball prowess was strong enough that he began offering lessons to new players, wanting both a way to share his knowledge and a reason to get out of the house. Before long, the athlete's coaching business grew so popular that balancing it with his full-time work became unmanageable, and in July of that year, he quit Deloitte to pursue professional pickleball full-time—both as a player and a coach.

"I realized that, look, I'll have a couple years as a player, but there's a lot of business opportunities in pickleball which fit my background as an accountant," Navratil explained of his thought process. "So even if I didn't make any prize money, I still figured there was good income to be made in pickleball, and it's a growing industry I wanted to have a foothold in as it takes off."

In December 2021, he teamed up with the Association of Pickleball Professionals (APP) Tour to create the APP Academy, a program providing pickleball clinics to players attending APP-hosted tournaments. On the court, he's spent the last several months racking up dozens of medals, closing major sponsorship deals, and becoming famous enough that fans now stop him at the airport for photos. He even pioneered a type of serve—called "the chain saw"—so reliably unreturnable that it's now been banned from use[2] by USA Pickleball (a fellow player, Morgan Evans, called it "diabolical").

If juggling two separate sides of pickleball is a challenge, though, he's an expert at not showing it; in fact, on our call, Navratil—wearing a sweatshirt bearing the name of Franklin Sports, one of his sponsors—seemed not just relaxed, but inspired, especially when the subject of the future came up.

"On the playing side, I want to become ranked world number one in singles," he told me, without a moment's hesitation. "And then on the business side, I want to be nationally recognized as a premier instructor across the country."

IRINA TERESCHENKO

Age: 36
Hometown: Moscow, Russia
Claim to Fame: Fifth-rated player in all three divisions

The very first thing that Irina Tereschenko told me when we got on the phone was that she only started playing pickleball by accident. Back in 2013, she was focused entirely on tennis (sense a pattern here?), having spent the last several years turning an accomplished stint as a top-ranked college athlete into a successful career coaching other professional-level players. When her friends invited her to play a game called pickleball, she agreed, but she didn't enjoy the experience and walked away feeling less than convinced.

After that, Tereschenko had no intention of picking up a paddle again—but one of her friends, a pro pickleball player named Chris Miller, was so sure she'd make a great player despite her disinterest that he secretly signed the two of them up for an upcoming tournament, even purchasing her flight and housing. When Tereschenko balked, he explained his plan. "He was like, 'If you win money, which I know you will, you can pay me back. And if not, don't worry about it,'" she remembered.

Intrigued but still skeptical, Tereschenko asked her other friends if Miller was trustworthy enough for her to feel comfortable agreeing to such a risky proposal. They assured her that he was, and so, after some consideration, she decided to take a leap of faith, flying out to Utah with Miller for the 2013 Tournament of Champions. There wasn't any time for training, so she was forced to learn the game's rules, scoring, and positioning on the spot. Thankfully, the athlete was a quick study—so quick, in fact, that she ended up taking home a gold medal. "Somehow I was able to win singles and paid Chris back," Tereschenko said.

As exciting as the victory was, though, it still took more time for her to get totally on board the pickleball train, despite Miller's best efforts. "He was trying to get me to play more tournaments, and I just kept blowing them off because there was no prize money," she explained. (At the time, the purses offered by even the biggest competitions were substantially less than they are today.)

Over the next few years, though, as the competitive pickleball world became more established, Tereschenko's interest grew, and she started devoting more of her time to the game. With Miller as her mentor, teaching her strategy and giving her advice on everything from choosing a partner to finagling sponsorship deals, the athlete slowly but surely made her way up the rankings. In both 2018 and 2019, Tereschenko brought home the top prize at pro tournaments alongside her doubles partner Lucy Kovalova; in 2020 she dominated women's singles at the PPA Grand Slam. To date, she's earned thirty-five career gold medals, including from the U.S. Open and Nationals, and has even played celebrity games with athletes like Andre Agassi and Andy Roddick.

Not that she's one to brag, though. Tereschenko is totally understated when talking about her formidable pickleball career, so much so that when I asked what the most life-changing effect of pickleball has been for her, her answer wasn't the titles or the fame, but something much more inconsequential: exercise. ("Because going to the gym is super boring," she added.)

Mostly, the athlete credited her success in the sport to keen observations of other players' techniques and training that prioritizes all aspects of her health. "After tournaments, you come home, and you're exhausted," Tereschenko explained, adding that she always takes a few days off from playing following a competition to recover mentally and physically. During that time, she'll rest and engage in other activities beneficial for her well-being (she has an eclectic group of interests that includes everything from snowboarding to poetry), so by the time the next tournament comes around, she'll be ready to practice and play at peak performance.

Much of Tereschenko's time off the court is spent deepening her involvement in the pickleball community, a fact that might have baffled her 2013 self. Like many other players, she's developed valued new friendships thanks to the game. Yet while pickleball may be what initially bonds them, she's more interested in her pals' other talents and interests, since the sport's recent growth means that its fans haven't devoted their entire lives to playing.

"How many tennis players are actually better in something else than in tennis?" Tereschenko asked rhetorically. "In pickleball, it's quite the opposite, especially at the amateur level. Most people who play, they're pros at something else."

That said, as a relatively early entry into game's pro space, she does love connecting with other players who were there during those less popular days. "The popularity of the sport, and the fact that we have more, better-quality tournaments and better players, have made all of us the veterans," she said. "It makes all of my experiences super exciting, just because they were at different stages and phases of the sport. To follow it on this journey of getting bigger, it's fantastic."

She's doing a huge part in keeping that growth going, too. In Russia, her home country, Tereschenko worked with local players to start their own pickleball federation, which was recognized by the IFP in July 2021. A few months before we spoke, she'd returned to Moscow to help promote the sport, play some games, and answer questions on professional pickleball life.

Her encouragement has had an undeniable impact, and not just in Russia; on a trip to Thailand not long ago, Tereschenko helped inspire several dozen residents to get into pickleball, after randomly encountering a player and chatting about how they could collaborate on growing the sport's popularity. Run-ins like those, she told me, create ripple effects: Now "I can send my friends from Hong Kong and Japan to go play tournaments in Thailand."

The pro herself frequently competes internationally, traveling to various tournaments for the opportunity to meet pickleball players from around the world. "It's kind of nice to go to Europe where not too many Americans go, especially pros, and play under the radar and just hang out with new people and make new friends," she explained.

At home in America, meanwhile, Tereschenko has a widespread fan base, which she said is because she's lived in enough states (Arizona, California, Washington, and Texas) to have supporters across the country—well, one half of it, at least. "I have to work on my East Coast," she told me with a laugh.

If winning over two dozen states takes some effort, that's no problem; the more difficult things are in pickleball, the better, according to Tereschenko. "If it wasn't challenging," she said, "it would be boring."

THE PICKLEBALL
COMMUNITY

In the spring of 2021, Beatriz Milito Maia, a sixty-year-old nurse from Chicago, had only been playing pickleball for a few months when she found herself dealing with one of the sports world's most dreaded problems: the yips. Hour after hour spent unsuccessfully trying to improve her serve had led to a sudden inability to accurately manage even one, and it had gotten to a point that she'd started to give up all hope. Frustrated and with her confidence low, Milito Maia thought a change of scenery might help, so she decided to switch to a different court. There, practicing her serves against a wall, she noticed

I now have really good friends in our state and probably ten more just through pickleball. Going to tournaments now is more like family reunions.

—Jay Wilson, 4.0-level player and pickleball ambassador

a younger woman nearby who seemed to be capably assisting a man with his shot technique. Desperate for help, Milito Maia walked over and asked the woman if she was a pickleball coach.

Unfortunately, she wasn't—the man was her husband, not a student. Still, "she gave me her number," Milito Maia recalled when we spoke in January, having met via that Facebook group for pickleball fans. Grateful but no more optimistic than before that she would ever fix her serve, she resumed practicing on the wall, to no avail. Later in the day, though, she heard her name called from across the court.

The woman, Milito Maia saw, was now playing with a friend, and despite the clear differences in their skill level from hers, they were inviting her to join. "I was touched that an obviously better player invited a total stranger who couldn't even serve to play with them," she recalled, adding that when she came over, they didn't hesitate to accommodate her abilities.

When she got home that evening, Milito Maia looked the woman up and discovered that her new friend wasn't just a more experienced player, but a professional one, having won several tournaments at the 5.0. level. Yet, to her amazement, this athlete had been more than happy to help out a total beginner for free.

After a few weeks, Milito Maia decided to call her up and ask for lessons. The pro said yes, and so they began meeting regularly on the court to conquer the newcomer's yips and improve her overall game. Each lesson also saw the two women learn more about each other's lives outside of pickleball. They discovered they had a lot in common, from their faith to their political views to their relationships with their husbands.

Over time, the duo connected more and more, and it didn't take long before their initial coach-student roles began to feel irrelevant. "Our relationship developed from pure business to true friends, confidantes, and motivators of each other whenever down," Milito Maia said.

Even when she broke her arm in the autumn, putting a pause on their lessons, the women's bond only deepened. Milito Maia's friend visited her often throughout her recovery, providing emotional support and comfort to the injured nurse.

It didn't even matter that, after Milito Maia's arm healed, winter had set in and so they couldn't resume their outdoor lessons. The twosome still talked every day, chatting about their shared interests and supporting each other whenever problems arose. "We know we can count on each other for whatever life threw at us," the newer player said. "Our friendship surpassed pickleball."

Today the women are closer than ever. And while Milito Maia's skills have improved immensely since that first lesson—she now plays in tournaments at the 3.5+ level—that's not what she values most about their bond. When she first started playing pickleball, she told me, she hadn't expected to make any friends from the game, noting that pickleball's social aspect was initially not her priority. Now, though, she couldn't feel more different. Thanks to pickleball, she said, "I made a special friend for life."

For countless players, pickleball has given them the chance to foster meaningful relationships with people whom they might not have gotten to know otherwise, but who share a common, deep love for the sport. Take Debra McCartan, a retired player and coach from Denver, Colorado, whom I also connected with through Facebook. When we spoke, she told me that being a part of the pickleball community has helped her cope with the 2016 death of her beloved husband, Jim. The couple had begun playing the game together after moving to a South Carolina neighborhood where pickleball was a popular pastime, and both husband and wife had instantly taken to the sport's mix of exercise and socialization, growing close to their playing partners. Sadly, Jim passed away just a year after their move, and "the grief and numbness were overwhelming," McCartan remembered.

Yet as she dealt with her pain, her pickleball friends and neighbors gathered around her for support, and when she decided to resume playing, they understood how badly she needed a distraction and made sure she got one. "When we were on the court, there was no talk of death, grief, or sadness, just pickleball," McCartan recalled. "My mind cleared, and for two hours, I was not the one whose husband just died, but Deb with a great backhand put-away shot."

In the time since then, the pickleball community has become a haven for her as she continues to heal, giving her the space she needs to focus solely on the game, not her grief. Today, nearly six years since Jim's death, the pickleball court is still "the only place where I can check my sadness at the gate," McCartan said.

On particularly difficult days, like Jim's birthday and the anniversary of his passing, McCartan makes sure to fit in several hours of play. The "wave of sadness and loss" still hits, she said, but pickleball makes handling those emotions far more manageable. "I don't think that after forty years of being with Jim, the grieving process will ever end, but I do know that this game and the people who play it have kept me moving forward," she said.

Other sports have their own communities, of course, and player friendships are not limited to pickleball. But every single player I've connected with agreed that there's just something about the way this game's world is that feels different. The pickleball community is a network full of players who, through their actions on and off the court, are committed to creating a support system for each other.

Often, friendships are built simply by walking onto an available court and introducing yourself to strangers. Places 2 Play,[1] a site (and app) run by USA Pickleball that contains info on the thousands of courts available worldwide, is an excellent resource to help players do just this. The database is consistently updated by more than 40,000 people, and around 110 new locations are added each month.

PicklePlay is another popular app that you can use to find not only available courts, but also clubs, events, and players located within a certain area. Tyson Apostol, the reality star and pickleball player, uses PicklePlay to find courts and let his fans know where he'll be. Often, *Survivor* fans aiming for a selfie will show up to his court despite no knowledge of the game, but Apostol, armed with extra paddles, will find himself teaching them pickleball basics. (Occasionally the app will even lead to him encountering former castmates on the court, including Rob "Boston Rob" Mariano and Gervase Peterson.) Even when he's just playing with strangers, though, Apostol appreciates the chance to get to know other players, and he's turned several of these opportunities into true friendships. "There are people I talk to regularly that I would never have even had in my life before pickleball," he said.

Facebook, too, has become a valuable resource for players looking to connect with each other. The social network is home to hundreds of pickleball groups where members can chat and connect, some of which are organized by location and others by age, gender, skill level, and more. Dave Gould, the player from Saratoga Springs, New York, joined a Facebook group for open play at his local park five years ago, after discovering the sport while on vacation and wanting to continue playing it back home. The group provided info on where and when to meet, and when Gould arrived at the location, he was astounded by how many other players had also shown up to play. "On a Saturday morning, all eight courts were full, with people waiting," he recalled.

As a former tennis and racquetball player, Gould was especially taken aback by the friendliness pickleball players showed toward each other, even during heated competitions. "In my other racquet sports, this social aspect was never present to this degree," he said.

The more time Gould spent playing, the more people he got to know, expanding his circle of friends and helping him become a better player in turn. "I have a solid eight to twelve players who could give me a run for my money any day of the week when we step on the court," he said of his current circle. "It's a beautiful thing to have that competition on hand."

With so many courts now open and tools now available for players to use, it's easier than ever to meet fellow pickleball fans simply by chance. But if you're looking for a more structured way of connecting with the bigger pickleball community, there are a few other options popular with players across the globe.

PICKLEBALL CLUBS

If your goal is to find a group of like-minded players to partner with or compete against, consider joining a pickleball club. There are hundreds of clubs in existence worldwide, often set up by nonprofessional fans of the sport and requiring no fees from their members, just a desire to come together and play. These clubs usually congregate at local rec centers or parks, and their members communicate info about pickleball meetups and events through their social media pages.

The USA Pickleball website has a constantly updated directory of pickleball clubs across both the United States and Canada, so you can search for your location and see what's available. If you don't find a club near you, consider starting one yourself![2] That may sound daunting, but all you would need to do is pick a location with available courts (temporary or permanent), advertise the club around your community, and create a schedule for meetups that others can access. Once things are up and going, add the club to that USA Pickleball list (for free) so anyone searching for a group based in your area can find it easily and join.

Clubs are also a great way to get information on local tournaments, as organizers will often advertise them on social media and answer questions from members considering signing up. Players interested in giving back to the pickleball community, too, can benefit from joining clubs, as there are always opportunities for members to volunteer at events, help provide equipment, and keep courts in pristine condition.

PICKLEBALL LEAGUES

For those who want not just to meet others through pickleball but to improve their skills, leagues are another solid choice. Like clubs, leagues consist of groups of players coming together for games, but *unlike* clubs, leagues are highly organized, with different levels based on skill level and frequently scheduled competitions. Leagues are typically seasonal (lasting several weeks or a few months at a time), and members pay fees that go toward expenses like equipment and prizes for winners.

While some of these groups, called team leagues, are based around factors like gender or age, many others use a ladder structure,[3] meaning that players of similar skill levels are placed on a "rung" each week, with the most advanced members at the top and the lowest-ranked ones at the bottom. The rankings are updated week by week, so players often go up or down a "rung" of the ladder depending on their performance, and the rankings are used to determine who should compete against whom in games.

A common ladder format used by many leagues is the round-robin, also known as a shoot-out. In this structure, four players with the same ranking are placed together on the ladder, and each of them spends the next several days playing doubles games against the other three in their group. When the scores are tallied, each player gets a chance to move individually up or down the ladder for the following week, with the goal, of course, of eventually moving to the highest rung. (Some larger leagues have multiple ladders to account for their greater number of players, with each ladder signifying a different rating range— such as 3.5–4.0– and allowing for players to move between ladders as needed.)

The Global Pickleball Network keeps an updated list of the more than 2,600 leagues[4] set up worldwide, providing their locations along with their type (team or ladder), number of players, and skill level required to join. And, like with clubs, you can always start your own pickleball league if you don't see one near you that fits what you're looking for—just make sure you're up for the responsibilities that come with organizing weekly games and extracting funding from members, among other tasks.

AMBASSADORS AND MORE

Even if you decide not to take part in a club or league, there are still several worthy ways to deepen your involvement with the sport. For one, you can become a member of USA Pickleball, joining more than 53,000 other players of various skill levels. Membership is required for any player participating in a USA Pickleball–sanctioned tournament, and if you want to get your official pickleball ranking, you'll need a membership to do so, too. There's an annual fee all members pay, but it goes toward funding and developing pickleball programs across the country, including in high schools and underserved communities.

Becoming a member also allows you to apply to be a pickleball ambassador,[5] or in other words, an official representative of the game in the area you live. There are hundreds of ambassadors throughout the country, organized under districts and across regions, who volunteer their time to promote pickleball in their town or city. Ambassadors may help organize clubs or leagues, or keep an eye out for new courts to add to the Places 2 Play database. You don't need to be a player at a specific skill level or have a certain amount of experience to take on this role; all that's required is that you love pickleball and want to share it with others in your community. The application to become an ambassador is available on the USA Pickleball site, as well as a list of ambassadors across the United States and a full listing of the job's responsibilities.

In the same Facebook group for pickleball fans that I used to connect with players like Beatriz Milito Maia and the wheelchair player Jamie Elliott, I was introduced to Jay Wilson, a pickleball ambassador who's also the executive director of a West Virginia faith-based nonprofit. When we chatted, he told me that he first discovered pickleball while on vacation at a resort several years ago, and that while he was no stranger to sports as a former racquetball, tennis, and basketball player, he was surprised by how quickly the pickleball "addiction" took hold. Before long, he was enrolling in clinics and camps, studying online tutorials, and spreading the word about the sport to anyone who would listen. Taking the next step to become an official ambassador—which required filling out an application and being interviewed by a higher-ranking pickleball official—just made sense.

"I suspect everybody I meet, no matter what the reason, I will ask them if they play pickleball, followed with, 'Are you ready to try it?'" Wilson told me.

Originally his ambassador territory was just one county in his home state, but recently, USA Pickleball increased his zone to cover all of West Virginia's southern counties. In his volunteer role, he works with as many pickleball clubs in the area as he can to recruit new players, keep the courts running smoothly, and direct local tournaments.

The work hasn't always been easy. In the summer of 2021, Wilson started a league in his own county with the aim of bringing on twenty new members, a lofty goal, considering "there were probably only eight people in our own county who played, and our group was five of them," as he recalled. Yet with some serious hustling, he not only reached his goal, but surpassed it; he ended up with thirty people playing in the new league and its season-ending tournament.

Wilson's passion for the game has rubbed off on those around him. He and his wife of thirty-one years, Karen, take to the courts daily for competitive games, and his twenty-seven-year-old son is also an avid player. The father-son duo have even competed together in a tournament, losing their final match to "two young hotshots" by a single point, per Wilson (he added that the image of the erroneous shot is forever embedded in his mind).

Pickleball is so integral to the sixty-two-year-old's life that he's become a referee, coach, and an equipment distributor for Gearbox, in addition to his role as an ambassador. Any time he can share his love for the sport with others, he jumps at the opportunity.

"[Karen and I] joke all the time that if we are not playing pickleball, we are thinking about pickleball, watching pickleball videos, talking about pickleball, or wishing we were doing any of those things," Wilson told me, sharing that his dream is to one day open a pickleball training and retreat center.

Many other ambassadors have similarly ambitious goals. Dan Beeman, an author and bed-and-breakfast owner from Palm Desert, California, whom I met via Facebook, told me over a phone call that he took on the role because he considers himself to be "an evangelist of pickleball." As an ambassador, he works to continually find ways to share the sport with as many newcomers that possible because, in his words, "the more people that hear about it and try it, the happier the world is."

In 2018, shortly after becoming an ambassador, Beeman organized a pickleball clinic for players in his area. With the help of a few local pro players and a paddle manufacturer who generously provided paddles, he spent the day teaching more than sixty beginners how to dink, serve, and volley. "It was a hugely successful event," he recalled.

Not long after, Beeman also developed the idea for a parent-child "Pickle Day" at his son's high school, inviting teens and their families to learn the basics and practice drills. The free event proved so popular with attendees—most of whom were brand-new to the sport—that it became an annual tradition. Over time, the curriculum has evolved more and more, with the 2021 Pickle Day including not just lessons but tournaments, contests, and picnic celebrations.

Beeman's son graduated in 2022, but the writer has no plans to stop hosting the event. "Everyone's always asking me, 'When's the next Pickle Day?'" he said. "It's grown each year, and people just have a blast."

From ambassadors introducing the game to families, to experienced players taking newcomers under their wing, the pickleball community is filled with members committed to making the sport's world bigger and better, one paddle at a time.

THE FUTURE
OF PICKLEBALL

As exciting as pickleball's massive growth in recent years has been, the most thrilling part of all is that the *real* explosion is likely just beginning. Over the next several years, as more money, attention, and players undoubtedly pour into the sport, fans can expect to see the pickleball landscape balloon with more courts, bigger tournaments, and greater recognition for the game's top pro players, among other changes.

Already, things are moving fast. At November 2021's PPA Masters, for example, there was such high attendance—and such high energy from the crowd—

So far, [pickleball's growth] has just been beyond our original expectations—far beyond. It feels like every day things could change, and you're just riding this wave of excitement.

—*Hannah Johns, head of content for the Professional Pickleball Association (PPA)* that multiple major brands signed on as sponsors just based on photos and videos posted on social media. According to Hannah Johns, the PPA's head of content, the organization scored some of its biggest sponsorship deals to date after that event, including with several brands that aren't pickleball-specific. This was clear proof that the mainstream world was starting to gain confidence in the game's potential, and a boon for pickleball itself, since non-endemic sponsors often have more money and resources to pour into everything from TV streaming deals to prize money to tournament venue size.

Sponsors aren't the only sign that pickleball's impact on the world is getting larger. Below are some of the many other indications that the sport is quickly becoming an integral part of our culture, from the rise of pickleball-themed restaurants to the creation of pickleball-centric tours overseas.

PICKLEBALL BARS, RESTAURANTS, AND REC CENTERS

Some of the biggest additions to America's pickleball landscape in recent years have been the creation of numerous restaurants, bars, and community centers themed around the game. In Texas, for instance, there's the Austin Pickle Ranch, a sports and entertainment facility featuring thirty-two courts, a music venue, and food trucks, in addition to areas for beach volleyball and yoga.[1] Over in Hanover, Massachusetts, you can walk into Pickles, a 25,000-square-foot facility with a viewing deck, snack bars, and stores filled with pickleball gear.[2] And if you live in Missouri, Texas, Kansas, and Oklahoma, you can claim a seat at the perfectly named Chicken N Pickle, a chain of restaurants/bars and courts founded several years ago by Dave Johnson, a player who wanted to combine his "love for delicious, wood-fired chicken and the game of pickleball," according to the company's site.[3] (In line with the sport's growth, two more Chicken N Pickle locations are already on the way.)

In coming years, expect to see many more businesses like these set up shop throughout the country, catering to both the skyrocketing market of pickleball fans and nonplaying (for now!) customers simply looking for some fun new places to try out.

PICKLEBALL VACATIONS

Pickleball tourism is another fast-growing industry, and a key component of the sport's exciting future. Every year, more and more players plan fun-filled vacations to areas like Palm Desert, California, or Myrtle Beach, South Carolina, hoping to take advantage of the locales' pickleball-centric offerings.

In Naples, Florida, for instance, home to the U.S. Open, fans come all year long to play on the esteemed courts and enjoy the city's bustling downtown and beautiful beaches. At the time cofounder Terri Graham and I spoke, the 2022 Championships were still three months away—yet the day before our phone call, she said, "there had to have been over six hundred people" taking up the park's sixty-four courts. "It's just amazing how many people fly in here to play here," she added.

Some pickleball fans have taken it upon themselves to create resources for players who love fitting the game into their travels. In 2021, Laura Gainor, the USA Pickleball marketing consultant, launched Pickleball in the Sun, an online source for pickleball destinations and experiences across the globe that acts as an extension to a monthly column in *Pickleball Magazine* she writes with the same focus. On the brand's site and social media pages, fans can find highlights on resorts and hotels that have ample pickleball courts, as well as info on non-pickleball activities to explore nearby during their getaways.

The brand was inspired by Gainor's own journey with pickleball and travel. When she first started playing back in 2019, she viewed it merely as a hobby (albeit an addictive one), setting up games in her family's driveway and facing off against friends at her local community center. Yet over the next two years, her love for pickleball grew so much that she began basing most of her travels around opportunities to play, purposefully picking resorts and hotels with nearby courts so she could fit in a few matches between sights. She wasn't alone in doing so; as pickleball's popularity soared, Gainor encountered more and more people who were similarly planning vacations and choosing lodging with the game at the forefront of their minds.

"I was like, 'Gosh, there's something here. Pickleball is more than just a sport—it's a lifestyle,'" she remembered thinking.

INTERNATIONAL PICKLEBALL TOURS

Some pickleball fans looking to make the most out of their passion even choose to head overseas to enjoy the game and bond with other players, using the international vacation packages centered on pickleball offered by a growing number of companies. Pickleball Getaways, for example, is run by top pro Ben Johns and Israeli player Dekel Bar and has organized past trips to places including the Mayan Riviera and Ecuador. The company has several expeditions to Europe in the works,[4] including a trip to Croatia, where travelers will spend ten days mixing in sightseeing and stays at four-star hotels with daily pickleball games and instruction.

There's also Pickleball Trips, which takes its customers as far as Thailand and Japan and promises exclusive travel adventures, as well as pickleball clinics taught by pros and events attended by local players.[5] (Unsurprisingly, these kinds of vacations don't come cheap; the average trip from either company costs a few thousand dollars per person.)

PICKLEBALL IN SCHOOLS

Although many schools around the United States already offer pickleball as part of their curriculum, it's not nearly as widespread as, say, tennis or badminton, and often not taught with the same level of knowledge or experience by instructors. When I spoke to USA Pickleball chief operating officer Justin Maloof, he told me that one of the organization's most pressing goals is to give schools more tools and resources around pickleball, thus enabling instructors to effectively teach the sport in a way that emphasizes its collaborative, enjoyable nature.

In 2021, USA Pickleball launched the Youth Program Provider (YPP), a pickleball teaching curriculum designed for maximum participation from students. Rather than each child waiting their turn to rotate into a game and barely getting any playing time, as typically happens in gym classes, they form small groups and participate in interactive "station work" before using the skills they've just learned in a game. The program, which costs forty dollars a year to join, also provides activity cards and videos to teachers to help them explain lessons and run drills, along with discounted equipment.[6] After a slow initial rollout due to the effects of the pandemic, USA Pickleball is now focused on spreading word of the YPP during 2022 and beyond.

PICKLEBALL ACROSS THE WORLD

Since 2019, the International Federation of Pickleball (IFP) has seen a 360 percent increase in its member countries, according to the organization, with heavyweights like South Korea and France joined by smaller nations like Malta, Belize, and even Tonga. Many of these countries have their own pickleball tournaments, and the IFP runs its own international competition, the Bainbridge Cup, at different locations around the world each year (at the time of writing, the 2022 host nation hadn't been announced). The APP also has several European stops on its upcoming tour schedule, including the French, English, and Spanish Opens.

Closer to home, in Canada, pickleball is also rapidly expanding. The PPA Tour already has one event on the 2022 roster in Toronto, and the goal, officials told me, is to soon add a stop in Montreal.

Steve Deakin, the pro player from Vancouver, said that while he believes the country is "a few years behind" the United States in terms of court availability and league participation, he's confident they'll catch up in no time. "I guarantee you, it's growing very quickly up here," he said, before teasing that he's involved with a few projects focused on Canadian's pickleball development.

Mexico, too, is steadily becoming a hotspot for the game, having joined the IFP in June 2021. That December, the country's federation held its first international pickleball tournament[7] in San Juan del Rio, Queretaro, and the APP Tour's 2022 lineup features both a Guadalajara and Cancun Open (the PPA plans to host its first Mexican tournaments in 2023). Meanwhile, on the lifestyle side of things, the Tres Palapas Baja Pickleball Resort in Los Barriles, Baja California Sur, promises to be "Mexico's number one pickleball destination" with weekly competitions and a seaside restaurant.[8]

PICKLEBALL IN THE OLYMPICS

For many fans of the sport, the biggest indication that pickleball's popularity is here to stay will be when it becomes an Olympic sport. In December 2021, USA Pickleball partnered with the Special Olympics, and the two organizations have big plans for pickleball's future inclusion in the games. While details of the deal were still being sorted out when Maloof and I spoke, he told me that both sides were "extremely excited" about the collaboration's potential. "For them to embrace pickleball and do it with us so that we can provide our resources and information and programming that they can integrate?" he said. "We feel it's gonna be huge."

In addition to Pickleball's inclusion in the Special Olympics, players and organizers have begun working hard in the last few years on a campaign for pickleball to join the 2028 official Olympic Games in Los Angeles.

Steve Sidwell, a player and ambassador, told the *Desert Sun* in a January interview that he joined the IFP largely to help increase pickleball's Olympic chances.[9] A sport needs to be played in at least seventy-five countries in order to officially qualify for inclusion in the Games; currently, pickleball currently counts sixty. But as Sidwell noted, the International Olympic Committee (IOC)'s decision often comes down more to financial factors like branding and audience, meaning that pickleball likely needs to have enough fans tuning in on TV to inspire major brands to buy sponsorships, thereby bringing serious money into the Games.

At the Los Angeles Games, Sidwell said, the IFP is planning to introduce pickleball on a smaller level to showcase its popularity and potential—but some officials believe that by 2024, the game will be widespread enough around the world that convincing the IOC may not even be needed.

"I do think there's a really good chance" of pickleball entering the Olympics, said Connor Pardoe, the PPA commissioner, when we spoke. "The professional leg of the sport needs to grow internationally, and it's just not really quite there yet, but do I think it can get there? Yeah."

Pro players, too, are thrilled about the possibility. When I asked the Moscow-born Irina Tereschenko, for instance, about her pickleball goals, she didn't hesitate before listing the Olympics as a top priority. The fact that she'll be well into her forties—older than most Olympic athletes—by the time 2028 comes around only added to the draw. "To be an Olympian at that age . . . chances like that don't really come often in life," she said.

Besides, Tereschenko added, the wait just means there's more time for her to become an even stronger player. "I'm still trying to get to the top of my game," she told me with her trademark confidence. "That's where pickleball and I are similar—we haven't peaked yet."

Indeed, with so many exhilarating changes for the game already happening and more being added to the docket every minute, there's likely no stopping pickleball from making it all the way to the top. Still, while the sport is undeniably spreading at warp speed right now, we can't *truly* know how far things will go, or if there will be a point not long from now when pickleball's numbers begin to slow.

David Jordan, the director for pickleball at the Huntsman World Senior Games and a former president of USA Pickleball, told me that while he thinks pickleball's rise won't end anytime soon, he does predict a shift in where, and how, the sport is played. "I think in the future, you're probably gonna have more league play and less tournament play," he mused, due to what he thinks may be an oversaturation of competition opportunities.

At the same time, though, Jordan added, the increased attention on pickleball's pros may lead to fewer resources for the game's casual players. "In several sports that you look back on—racquetball, tennis—the professional side of it pretty much drowned out the recreational side of it, and the numbers started to drop off in recreational," he noted. "I hope that doesn't happen with pickleball, but I could see that possibly taking place."

There's no way to know for sure, but luckily, there are plenty of players whose enthusiasm for the sport and desire to see it grow are successfully keeping both sides of pickleball alive and well. Thanks to all of them—and all of you—pickleball's future is looking brighter by the second.

CONCLUSION

ven if you started out this book as a total beginner who'd just recently gotten into playing pickleball, by now you've gained enough insight on the sport to be no less than an expert. You know how the game started (if not *exactly* how it got its name), and the difference between a dink and a drive; you know what equipment to buy, and how to set up a court; you know what to look for in a coach, and which strategies to hone and use; you know how to enter tournaments, and what it's like to go pro; and, last but not least, you know how to get involved in the sport's community, and what exciting work is being done to enable pickleball's continued growth.

Pickleball has been a central force in my life. It has helped relieve my stressors at work, created friendships for life, improved my mental and physical health, given me confidence, and channeled my competitive spirit.

—Ruth Rosenquist, 4.0-level player, marketing consultant, and director for the IFP

You also know the stories of dozens of players and organizers whose lives have been impacted for the better due to pickleball. You read about kids like Jack Loughridge, who have proven to themselves that they're strong enough to take on athletes four times their age. You met coaches like Joe Borrelli and Tracie Holmes, who have found renewed purpose and drive by helping others feel confident on the court. You learned from pros like Catherine Parenteau and Steve Deakin, who have worked tirelessly to overcome challenges to achieve their dreams. You heard from organizers like Connor Pardoe and Laura Gainor, who have taken huge risks and changed their careers in order to aid pickleball's growth. And you got to know many other players like Beatriz Milito Maia and Debra McCartan and Cynthia Etheridge, people who have forged relationships with strangers on the court that have turned into valued, lifelong friendships.

My hope is that these stories have given you a window into both how much passion players have for pickleball and the enormous impact it's had on their lives. It's enough to make you want to celebrate the sport and the happiness it fosters—and if this is the case, and you want to include more pickleball in your own life, here are a few options for doing just that.

PICKLEBALL PARTIES

Got a celebration coming up? Consider hosting a pickleball party, an event featuring décor, snacks, costumes, and more themed around the game. (Jack Loughridge, for example, was planning a glow-in-the-dark pickleball birthday party at the time we spoke, just as long as his mother managed to figure out how to set up blacklights in their backyard. "I'm working on it," she told me with just a hint of panic in her voice.)

If you need some inspiration for how to plan a pickleball party, I've got you covered.

FOOD/DRINK IDEAS
- Pickles (duh!)
- Pickleback shots (for those blissfully unaware: shots of bourbon or whiskey immediately followed by shots of pickle brine)
- Paddle-shaped cakes
- Court-shaped charcuterie boards
- Ball- or paddle-shaped cookies

DÉCOR IDEAS
- Green, white, and yellow everything!
- Centerpiece vases filled with balls
- Signs saying "please dink responsibility" or "don't dink and drive"
- Wreaths made of balls

ACTIVITY IDEAS

- Reserve a local court for a mini tournament, or create a court in your driveway
- Book a stay at a hotel/resort with courts for a few friends
- Hire a local coach to teach a group lesson
- Watch a tournament on TV together

GIFT IDEAS

- Goody bags filled with balls
- Makeshift trophies or medals
- Pickleball-themed socks, hats, or tote bags (more on that below!)

PICKLEBALL MERCH

Of course, you don't have to wait until a special occasion to express your love of pickleball. From clothing to jewelry, artwork to toys, being a fan of the sport and appreciating its benefits has never been easier.

Most major pickleball-specific sites now offer clothing and accessories themed to the sport, so you can show off your pride; on Pickleball Central, for example, you can buy everything from a mug saying "coffee now, pickleball later" to a pack of hair ties emblazoned with tiny pastel paddles.

It's not just sports-centric retailers getting in on the moment, though. On Etsy, where homemade products reign supreme, there are thousands of options for pickleball tote bags, stickers, and wineglasses, not to mention a truly excellent collection of hand-made artwork (I'm particularly fond of a watercolor print featuring two visor-wearing pickles having it out on the court).

PICKLEBALL MAGAZINES

For those looking to embrace their love of pickleball in a different way, there are also now a number of magazines that cover the sport exclusively.

Pickleball Magazine, the most well-known of the bunch with more than 100,000 readers per issue,[1] takes a more advice-centered approach, offering an abundance of tips, strategies, and instructional demonstrations.

Its newer competitor *InPickleball,* meanwhile, which launched in 2021, is more focused on the lifestyle element of the game, and aimed at a readership with a surplus of both time and money to pour into the game. In July 2021, right before its launch, the magazine's publishers told the *New York Post* that they intended *InPickleball* to be "the *Vogue* of Pickleball,"[2] and with editions featuring elaborate recipes, resort spotlights, and glossy photo shoots with celebrity players like *Real Housewives* star Teddi Mellencamp, it's certainly living up to that mission.

PICKLEBALL PODCASTS

The pickleball craze hasn't just spread to print media. Podcasts, too, have quickly adapted to the game's fast-growing popularity, with dozens of options offering subscriptions for fans. Some of these podcasts primarily tackle news and updates surrounding the sport, while others focus on interviews with players, or tips from tournaments; many are hosted by current or former pros themselves.

In the fall of 2021, Tyson Apostol, the *Survivor* alum and pickleball superfan, teamed up with Thomas Shields, founder of the pickleball website The Dink, to launch *PicklePod,* a weekly show featuring commentary on the sport from the duo and a (relatively) famous guest. Although the men were aware of their considerable competition in the pickleball podcast space before launching, they hoped *PicklePod* would offer something different for listeners due to its hosts' unique backgrounds.

"[Shields's] operation at The Dink is all about following everything in pickleball, updating everybody on the latest news and all the happenings and tournament standings, so he brings all that knowledge," Apostol told me. "And then I bring all the casual knowledge and the fun and personality." (Being close enough friends with many of the game's pros, like Zane Navratil and Rob Nunnery, to ask them on the show doesn't hurt, he added.)

While no numbers were shared, Apostol said that the show has earned a devoted following in the short time since its debut; perhaps the biggest sign of its success, he noted, is that when fans stop him on the street to mention that they listen to one of his podcasts (he has two others, about *Survivor* and news), *PicklePod* now comes up most often.

From parties to podcasts, clothing to magazines, there are more ways than ever before for pickleball players to infuse our affection for the game in all aspects of our lives. As for why we choose to? Well, that's easy— pickleball has changed us for the better, and we want the world to know.

It's certainly been the case for me. When I first picked up that paddle, I could never have imagined just how big an effect the game would end up having on my life. But from the connections I've made, to the opportunities I've been granted, to the self-assurance I've gained, pickleball has brought more positives to my universe than I can count.

The more immersed I become in the pickleball world, the bigger my community becomes. Just recently, for example, former classmates whom I hadn't spoken to in years reached out to tell me how much they, too, loved the game, leading to renewed friendships. Similarly, sweet but shy neighbors whom I didn't previously know well opened up not long ago to share that they hoped I'd one day teach them to play on our local courts (an offer I gladly, if nervously, accepted).

To millions of players like myself, pickleball is far more than just a sport. It's a community, a support system, a lifeline. It's a world full of warm, inclusive people who may differ in age, background, and experience level, but who are connected by their love of the game.

And if it didn't already, that world now includes you. From all of us: welcome.

ACKNOWLEDGMENTS

I couldn't have written *Pickleball for All* without the help and support of so many people, including:

- **Maddie Pillari,** my editor, whose incisive, spot-on notes made me a stronger writer and storyteller.
- **Lisa Sharkey, Emilia Marroquin, and the rest of the HarperCollins team,** who championed my ideas and provided countless vital insights of their own.
- **Andrew Blauner,** my agent, whose faith in me and excitement over this project have never wavered.
- **Nicole Fisher,** who offered invaluable guidance and friendship as I navigated the first-time-author trenches of contracts, covers, and more.
- **Laura Gainor,** who not only shared her own inspiring pickleball story, but crucially

connected me with dozens of other players and organizers.

- **Joe Borrelli,** who generously donated his time to give me a (much-needed) pickleball lesson.

- **The rest of the wonderful pickleball community who spoke to me for this book,** from pros to amateurs, coaches to ambassadors, organizers to commissioners.

- **The teachers and students at Redbud and Gotham,** whose understanding about my crazed schedule during the writing process was hugely appreciated.

- **My friends in New York, Raleigh, and across the country,** who cheered me on every step of the way and are generally just the best people.

- **Betsy and Gary Beyer,** whose gift of pickleball equipment in April 2020 was the catalyst for so much to come.

- **My parents, Joel and Lisa Simon,** whose love, support, and advice never failed to push me forward (the cookie cake didn't hurt, either).

- **And finally, Kurt,** who for five and a half years has been my closest friend, greatest champion, and steadiest force. I'm so grateful to spend my lifetime with you.

GLOSSARY

ACE—A serve that isn't returned by your opponent.

AMBASSADOR—A pickleball player designated by USA Pickleball to be an official representative of the game.

APP—The Association of Professional Pickleball, one of two major tours for the sport.

BACKCOURT—The area inside the court near the baseline.

BACKHAND—A shot in which you hit the ball using the back of your hand, on the opposite side of your dominant forehand.

BACKSPIN—Striking the ball with high-to-low motion, causing it to spin in the opposite direction of its path (also called "Chop" or "Slice").

BASELINE—The line at the back end of the court on each side.

CARRY—A shot where the ball is carried along the face of the paddle in forward motion.

CENTERLINE—The line extending from the Kitchen to the baseline, dividing the court into two equal halves.

CHOP—See: *Backspin*.

CROSS-COURT—The court area diagonally opposite your side court.

DEAD BALL—A ball declared after a fault, when the point is over.

DINK—A shot that arcs over the net and lands in your opponents' Kitchen.

DOUBLE BOUNCE—A ball that bounces more than once before being returned (resulting in a lost point).

DOUBLES—Games played between four people total, with two people on each team (men, women, or mixed).

DOUBLE ELIMINATION—A tournament format in which you have to lose twice before you're eliminated (you move to a consolation bracket after the first loss).

DRILLS—Repetitive exercises to build muscle memory and hone specific skills.

DRIVE—A straight and low shot that lands deep in your opponents' backcourt.

DROP SHOT—A shot that clears the net and lands in front of your opponents (also known as Third Shot Drop).

DROP SPIN—A shot that purposefully drops sharply after it crosses the net.

FACE—The surface of either side of the paddle, used to hit the ball.

FAULT—An action that violates a pickleball rule and stops play.

FOLLOW-THROUGH—The continuing forward motion of your swing as the ball leaves the paddle.

FOREHAND—A shot hit from the same side of your body as you're holding the paddle.

GAME—Play that goes until one team has reached 11 points, winning by two points.

GRIP—The way you hold the paddle handle in your hand (also, the material that's wrapped around the handle to provide cushioning).

GROUND STROKE—A ball that's hit after one bounce.

HALF VOLLEY—A shot hit immediately after the ball bounces and before it reaches maximum height.

IFP—The International Federation of Pickleball, the sport's international governing body.

JUNIOR—A pickleball player between the ages of seven and nineteen.

KITCHEN—The seven-foot non-volley zone in front of the net on both sides (also known as the Non-Volley Zone).

LET—A serve that hits the net, landing in the service court.

LINE CALLS—Verbal statements that indicate if a ball is in or out of bounds.

LOB—A shot that sends the ball up high and lands deep.

MATCH—A series of three games, typically (the number can vary).

MIDCOURT—The area on the court between the Kitchen and the baseline.

MIXED DOUBLES—Games played with both male and female players on each team.

NON-VOLLEY ZONE—See: *Kitchen*.

OPEN FACE—A shot hit with the paddle tilted slightly upward.

OVERHEAD SMASH—A powerful, overhand shot aimed downward into your opponents' court (often as a return to a high shot).

POACH—To cross over to your partner's side of the court and steal a shot.

PPA—The Professional Pickleball Association, one of two major tours for the sport.

PUT-AWAY—A shot that has no chance of being returned by your opponent.

RALLY—Game play that starts from the time the ball is served and ends when there's a fault.

RATING—The two-digit number given to players to assess their skill levels, typically between 1.0 and 5.0.

READY POSITION—Standing with your paddle in front of your body at chest height, with knees slightly bent and feet ready to move.

RECEIVER—The player diagonally opposite from the server, who'll return the serve.

ROUND ROBIN—A tournament format in which every player or team competes against every other player or team.

SERVE—An underhand stroke that puts the ball in play.

SERVER NUMBER—The number (1 or 2) indicating which teammate is serving at that moment in doubles.

SERVICE COURT—The area on either side of the centerline between the Kitchen line, baseline, and sideline.

SIDELINE—The line on each side of the court separating the playing zone from the out-of-bounds area.

SIDE OUT—When one team loses the serve, giving the opponents the chance to serve.

SINGLES—Games played between two people, with one player on each side.

SLICE—See: *Backspin.*

STROKE—The motion of hitting the ball with the paddle.

THIRD SHOT DROP—See: *Drop Shots.*

TOPSPIN—Putting spin on the ball from low to high, therefore causing it to spin in the same direction as it flies.

TWO-BOUNCE RULE—A rule stating that after the ball is served, the receiving team must let it bounce before returning, then the serving team must also let it bounce before returning. After both returns, the ball can be volleyed.

UNFORCED ERROR—A missed point that is due to your own fault, not your opponent's skill or strategy.

USA PICKLEBALL—The sport's American governing body.

VOLLEY—Hitting the ball in the air mid-rally before it bounces.

NOTES

1. "Pickleball Participation Report 2021," SFIA, accessed February 6, 2022, https://www.sfia.org/reports/949_Pickleball -Participation-Report-2021.

2. "Atlantic City Goes for Indoor Pickleball Record with New Tourney," *Press of Atlantic City,* accessed February 13, 2022, https://pressofatlanticcity.com/news/local/atlantic-city-goes-for -Indoor-pickleball-record-with-new-tourney/article 8b4a6400 -7f94-11ec-9458-4ff471539db3.html.

3. "About the IFP," IF Pickleball, accessed February 6, 2022, https://www.ifpickleball.org/about-ifp.

CHAPTER 1: HOW IT BEGAN

1. "History of the Game," USA Pickleball, accessed February 6, 2022, https://usapickleball.org/what-is-pickleball/history-of-the -game/.

2. "How Pickleball Really Got Its Name," *Pickleball Magazine,* accessed February 6, 2022, https://www.pickleballmagazine .com/pickleball-articles/How-Pickleball-Really-Got-Its-Name!

3. "On the Water: In a Pickle Explaining Pickle Boats," *Press Telegram,* accessed February 6, 2022, https://www .presstelegram.com/2021/04/02/on-the-water-in-a-pickle -explaining-pickle-boats/.

4. "The Doggone Lies About Pickleball," Puget Sound Blogs, accessed February 6, 2022, http://pugetsoundblogs.com

/bainbridge-conversation/2009/01/16/the-doggone-lies-about
-pickleball/.

5. "Pickleball 411: How the Game Got Its Name," Pickleball
   Channel, accessed February 6, 2022, https://www
   .pickleballchannel.com/name-of-game.

6. "The History of Pickleball," Onix Pickleball, accessed February 6,
   2022, https://www.onixpickleball.com/blogs/learn-pickleball
   /the-history-of-pickleball.

7. "4 Game Changers You Need to Know," *Pickleball Magazine,*
   accessed February 6, 2022, https://www.pickleballmagazine
   .com/tips-lessons/4-Game-Changers-You-Need-to-Know.

8. "Can You Recall the History of Pickleball Composite Paddles?
   Steve Can!" Pickleball Central, accessed February 6, 2022,
   https://blog.pickleballcentral.com/2015/02/.

9. "History," U.S. Open Pickleball Championship, accessed
   February 6, 2022, https://usopenpickleballchampionship.com
   /history.html.

10. "Pickleball Participation Report 2016," SFIA, accessed February
    6, 2022, https://www.sfia.org/reports/507_Pickleball
    -Participation-Report-2016.

11. "Guidelines for the Pickleball Hall of Fame," Pickleball Hall of
    Fame, accessed February 6, 2022, https://pickleballhalloffame
    .com/about-foundation/.

12. "Pickleball," Raleigh NC, accessed February 5, 2022, https://
    raleighnc.gov/pickleball.

13. "Can't Reserve a Pickleball Court? The Data Shows You Are Not
    Alone," *San Francisco Chronicle,* accessed February 13, 2022,
    https://www.sfchronicle.com/bayarea/article/Can-t
    -reserve-a-pickleball-court-The-data-show-16832958.php.

CHAPTER 2: PICKLEBALL 101

1. "How to Play Pickleball," USA Pickleball, accessed January 12,
   2022, https://usapickleball.org/what-is-pickleball/how-to-play/.

2. "How to Play Pickleball," Pickleball Inc, accessed January
   12, 2022, https://www.pickleball.com/rules-how-to-play
   -pickleball-s/106.htm.

3. "The Pickleball Kitchen," Amazin Aces, accessed January 12,
   2022, https://www.amazinaces.com/blogs/news/the-pickleball
   -kitchen-what-is-it-and-why-is-it-called-the-kitchen.

4. "Adaptive/Wheelchair Pickleball," USA Pickleball, accessed
   February 7, 2022, https://usapickleball.org/play/wheelchair
   -pickleball/.

5. "USA Pickleball Rulebook," USA Pickleball, accessed January 12, 2022, https://usapickleball.org/docs/ifp/USA-Pickleball-Rulebook.pdf.

CHAPTER 3: COURTS AND EQUIPMENT

1. "How to Make a Pickleball Court at Home in 5 Minutes with Chalk or Tape," Pickleball Portal, accessed January 18, 2022, https://www.pickleballportal.com/blog/diy-pickleball-courts/.

2. "Pickleball Paddles: Read This Before You Buy Your Next Paddle," Pickleball Portal, accessed January 18, 2022, https://www.pickleballportal.com/gear/paddles/pickleball-paddles-the-complete-buyers-guide/.

3. "The Difference Between Indoor and Outdoor Pickleballs," Pickleball University, accessed January 17, 2022, https://www.pickleballuniversity.com/home/the-difference-between-indoor-and-outdoor-pickleballs.

4. "Indoor vs Outdoor Pickleballs: Is There a Difference?" Pickleball Pulse, accessed January 17, 2022, https://pickleballpulse.com/indoor-vs-outdoor-pickleballs/.

5. "Selecting the Best Pickleball Net," Pickleball Land, accessed January 17, 2022, https://pickleball.land/selecting-the-best-pickleball-net/.

6. "Pickleball Court Lighting," Access Features, accessed January 18, 2022, https://www.accessfixtures.com/pickleball-court-lighting-packages/.

CHAPTER 4: GROWING YOUR GAME

1. "Find a Pickleball Teacher Near You," Pickleball Teachers, accessed January 24, 2022, https://www.pickleballteachers.com/.

2. "Pickleball Lessons, Teachers, and Coaches," Pickleball Central, accessed January 24, 2022, https://www.pickleballcentral.com/Pickleball_Coach_Instructor_s/210.htm.

3. "2022 Camps and Clinics," LevelUp Pickleball, accessed January 24, 2022, https://www.leveluppickleballcamps.com/.

4. "Camps," Engage Pickleball, accessed January 24, 2022, https://engagepickleball.com/pages/camps.

5. "CoachME Pickleball," CoachME Pickleball, accessed January 24, 2022, https://www.coachmepickleball.com/.

6. "Online Pickleball Video Lessons—Play Better Pickleball," The Pickler, accessed January 24, 2022, https://thepickler.com/products/online-pickleball-video-lessons.

7. "The Drop Shot Masterclass," Drop Shot Masterclass, accessed January 24, 2022, http://dropshotmasterclass.com/.

CHAPTER 5: STRATEGY

1. "7 Fun Drills to Use for Pickleball Practice," Pickleball Kitchen, accessed January 24, 2022, https://pickleballkitchen.com/7-fun-drills-to-use-for-pickleball-practice/.

2. "6 Types of Pickleball Exercises Every Player Should Do," Pink Pickleball, accessed January 24, 2022, https://pinkpickleball.com/pickleball-exercises/.

3. "13 Excellent Pickleball Drills for Beginners," Pickleball Drive, accessed January 27, 2022, https://pickleballdrive.com/13-excellent-pickleball-drills-for-beginners/.

4. "4 Essential Pickleball Skill Drills," Pickleball University, accessed January 24, 2022, https://www.pickleballuniversity.com/home/4-essential-pickleball-skill-drills.

5. "7 Fun Drills to Use for Pickleball Practice," Pickleball Kitchen, accessed January 20, 2022, https://pickleballkitchen.com/7-fun-drills-to-use-for-pickleball-practice/.

6. "Strategies—Doubles Strategies," USA Pickleball, accessed January 20, 2022, https://usapickleball.org/what-is-pickleball/how-to-play/strategies/doubles-strategies/.

7. "11 Best Pickleball Strategies & Tips to Improve Your Game as a Beginner," Racket Sports World, accessed January 20, 2022, https://racketsportsworld.com/best-pickleball-strategies-for-beginners/.

8. "25 Simple Pickleball Tips for Beginners," The Volley Llama, accessed January 20, 2022, https://thevolleyllama.com/pickleball-tips-for-beginners/.

9. "Pickleball Drop Shot," Pickleball Max, accessed January 21, 2022, https://www.pickleballmax.com/2020/04/pickleball-drop-shot/.

10. "Want to Play High Percentage Pickleball? Then Avoid These Shots!" The Pickler, accessed February 9, 2022, https://thepickler.com/blogs/pickleball-blog/high-percentage-pickleball.

CHAPTER 6: COMPETITIONS

1. "Description of USAP Approved Formats," USA Pickleball, accessed February 9, 2022, https://usapickleball.org/tournaments/approved-formats/.

2. "Pickleball Points: Margaritaville National Championships Return to Indian Wells," *Desert Sun*, accessed February 1, 2022, https://www.desertsun.com/story/sports/2021/12/02/pickleball-margaritaville-national-championships-return-indian-wells/8843881002/.

3. "Definitions of Player Skill Ratings," USA Pickleball, accessed January 31, 2022, https://usapickleball.org/tournaments/tournament-player-ratings/player-skill-rating-definitions/.

4. "Guide," Pickleball Tournaments, accessed February 10, 2022, https://www.pickleballtournaments.com/quickguide_player.pl.

5. "Pickleball Tournament Tips," The Pickler, accessed February 2, 2022, https://thepickler.com/blogs/pickleball-blog/pickleball-tournament-tips.

6. "Preparing for Your First Pickleball Tournament: 7 Steps," Pickleballer, accessed February 2, 2022, https://pickleballer.com/preparing-for-your-first-pickleball-tournament-7-keys-to-success/.

CHAPTER 7: GOING PRO

1. "APP Tour and Intersport Join Forces to Grow Pickleball," APP Tour, accessed February 13, 2022, https://apptour.org/app-tour-and-intersport-join-forces-to-grow-pickleball/.

2. "Pickleball Points: New Rules for 2022," *Desert Sun*, accessed February 2, 2022, https://www.desertsun.com/story/sports/2022/01/07/new-pickleball-rules-2022-no-chainsaw-serves-no-earbuds/9112720002/.

CHAPTER 8: THE PICKLEBALL COMMUNITY

1. "Places 2 Play," USA Pickleball, accessed January 30, 2022, https://usapickleball.org/play/places-2-play/.

2. "How to Set Up a Local Pickleball Club," Pickleball Central, accessed January 30, 2022, https://blog.pickleballcentral.com/2016/05/03/how-to-set-up-a-local-pickleball-club/.

3. "Pickleball Ladders—Are They Popular at Your Club?" Pickleball Max, accessed January 30, 2022, https://www.pickleballmax.com/2018/12/pickleball-ladders/.

4. "Pickleball Leagues Worldwide," Global Pickleball Network, accessed January 30, 2022, https://www.globalpickleball.network/pickleball-leagues/leagues.

5. "USA Pickleball Ambassadors," USA Pickleball, accessed January 30, 2022, https://usapickleball.org/get-involved/usa-pickleball-ambassadors/.

CHAPTER 9: THE FUTURE OF PICKLEBALL

1. "About Us," Austin Pickle Ranch, accessed February 4, 2022, https://www.austinpickleranch.com/.

2. "About Us," Pickles NE, accessed February 4, 2022, https://www.picklesne.com/about-us.

3. "Our Story," Chicken N Pickle, accessed February 4, 2022, https://chickennpickle.com/.

4. "Destinations," Pickleball Getaways, accessed February 5, 2022, https://www.pickleballgetaways.com/vacations.

5. "Trips," Pickleball Trips, accessed February 5, 2022, https://pickleballtrips.com/trips/.

6. "Youth Program Provider (YPP)," USA Pickleball, accessed February 5, 2022, https://usapickleball.org/memberships/ypp-membership-page/.

7. "New Dates: 2021 Mexico Pickleball National Tournament," Pickleball Tournaments, accessed February 5, 2022, https://www.pickleballtournaments.com/tournamentinfo.pl?tid=4852.

8. "About Us," Tres Palapas Baja, accessed February 5, 2022, https://trespalapasbaja.com/about-us/.

9. "Pickleball Points: When Will Our Sport Be in the Olympics?" *Desert Sun*, accessed February 5, 2022, https://www.desertsun.com/story/sports/2022/01/28/when-pickleball-included-olympics-paris-2024-l-a-2028/9257583002/.

CONCLUSION

1. "About Us," *Pickleball Magazine,* accessed February 4, 2022, https://www.pickleballmagazine.com/about.

2. "Pickleball Craze Inspires New Lifestyle Magazine," *New York Post,* accessed February 5, 2022, https://nypost.com/2021/07/20/pickleball-craze-inspires-new-lifestyle-magazine/.

RESOURCES

PicklePod (podcast)

Pickleball Kitchen (podcast)

Pickleball After Dark (podcast)

Pickleball Therapy (podcast)

Pickleball Channel—PickleballChannel.com

COMMUNITY

Places 2 Play—Places2Play.org (or app)

PicklePlay—PicklePlay.com (or app)

The Dink—TheDinkPickleball.com

The Pickler—ThePickler.com

Pickleball University—PickleballUniversity.com

EQUIPMENT

Pickleball Galaxy—PickleballGalaxy.com

Pickleball Central—PickleballCentral.com

Picky Pickleball—PickyPickleball.com

Pickleball Portal—PickleballPortal.com

Onix Pickleball—OnixPickleball.com

Selkirk Sport—Selkirk.com

Pickle-Ball Inc.—Pickleball.com

Paddletek Pickleball—Paddletek.com

HEAD—Head.com

Franklin Sports—FranklinSports.com

TRAVEL

Pickleball Trips—PickleballTrips.com

Pickleball Getaways—PickleballGetaways.com

Pickleball World Tours—PickleballWorldTours.com

Pickleball in the Sun—PickleballintheSun.com

ABOUT THE AUTHOR

Rachel Simon has written for the *New York Times, Glamour,* Vice, NBC News, Vulture, and more. Previously, she was an editor at Bustle, HelloGiggles, and Mic. When not writing, she teaches at Gotham Writers Workshop and Redbud Writing Project and creates custom crossword puzzles through her Etsy business, YourCrossword. A graduate of Emerson College and a New York native, she lives in Raleigh, North Carolina, with her husband, dog, and cat. You can find her on Twitter (@rachel_simon) and at rachelsimon.blog.